The Independent Working Musician

The Complete Guide
to Do-It-Yourself Success
in the Music Business

By Mary Cosola

Edited by Gino Robair

6400 Hollis Street
Emeryville, CA 94608

PRIMEDIA
Intertec

© 1998 PRIMEDIA Intertec Publishing

Library of Congress Catalog Card Number: 98-67690

Cover Design: Linda Gough
Book Design and Layout: Linda Gough
Production Staff: Mike Lawson, publisher; Gino Robair, editor

Authors of original Working Musician columns that were used in their entirety or in part in this book:
Michael Aczon, Camran Afsari, Michael Brown, Nadine Condon, Mary Cosola, Teri Danz, Karen Dere, Anne Eickelberg, Mike Levine, Michael Molenda, Jeff Obee, Cat Taylor.

6400 Hollis St., Suite 12
Emeryville, CA 94608
(510) 653-3307

Also from EMBooks:
Making the Ultimate Demo
Tech Terms: A Practical Dictionary for Audio and Music Production
Making Music With Your Computer

Also from MixBooks:
The AudioPro Home Recording Course, Volumes 1 and 2
I Hate the Man Who Runs This Bar!
How to Make Money Scoring Soundtracks and Jingles
The Art of Mixing: A Visual Guide to Recording, Engineering, and Production
500 Songwriting Ideas (For Brave and Passionate People)
Music Publishing: The Real Road to Music Business Success, Rev. and Exp. 4th Ed.
How to Run a Recording Session
Mix Reference Disc, Deluxe Ed.
The Songwriters Guide to Collaboration, Rev. and Exp. 2nd Ed.
Critical Listening and Auditory Perception
Keyfax Omnibus Edition
Modular Digital Multitracks: The Power User's Guide
Concert Sound
Sound for Picture
Music Producers
Live Sound Reinforcement

EMBooks is a division of PRIMEDIA Intertec Publishing

Printed in Auburn Hills, MI

ISBN 0-87288-6875

Dedication

Dedicated to Kevin Jackson, Drew Jackson,
Tony Cosola, Patricia Cosola, Shirley Jackson, and
Dick Jackson for supporting me, loving me,
and understanding the amount of work that went
into this book.

Contents

Section 3

Taking Care of Business: Personal career advice for musicians, from running your own studio to financing your band.

Section 4

The Fine Print: Important legal details every musician should know.

Introduction

Let's get one thing out of the way at the outset. This book will not make you a star. We do not guarantee you massive success and wealth in the music industry. That's up to you. Here's what we *are* giving you. We are giving you the insight, education, and tools you need to make your way through the music-business maze.

No matter what your musical goals are—maybe you *do* want that million-dollar record deal, or perhaps you want to establish your own label and completely do it yourself—the only way to truly be a success is to be in control of your career. One way to take control is to arm yourself with knowledge and advice from those that have been there. That's where *The Independent Working Musician* can help you.

We have drawn on more than six years worth of *Electronic Musician* "Working Musician" columns to demystify the often harrowing business of making a living as a musician. In the next 144 pages, we'll look at every aspect of making your way in the music business: collaboration, deal shopping, music-business law, promoting your own release, music publishing, running a label, and so on.

And believe me, I am not taking full credit for the abundant and helpful information on these pages. Many authors have contributed to this column over the years and therefore to this anthology. I'd like to single out two in particular for thanks and praise. First is Michael Molenda, former editor-in-chief of *Electronic Musician.* Before becoming editor, Mike championed the idea for the "Working Musician" column and is responsible for bringing it to the pages of *EM.* He established the column's direction and nurtured its success for two years before handing over the "Working Musician" reins to me. The second person I'd like to thank is San Francisco Bay Area entertainment attorney Michael Aczon. Michael has contributed many columns to "Working Musician" over the years, and his knowledge of the industry's legal and business intricacies never ceases to amaze. I have learned much from him over the years, as have the readers of *Electronic Musician.* In fact, almost all the chapters in the book's last section, "The Fine Print," were written by Michael.

So, read on and learn how to tackle the music business on your own terms.

—*Mary Cosola*

1

Significant Others

Developing and Maintaining Some of the Crucial Relationships in Your Music Career

CHAPTER 1

Collaboration Without Combat

ere's a conundrum for you: You need people to initiate collaboration, but people often make collaboration impossible. The inability to work toward a common goal is especially virulent in artistic communities, where many creative minds suffer from a lack of democratic neurons. The irony is that most collaborative efforts turn out more impressive results than do one-person studio acts.

Of course, ego is a powerful force, but it's not the only demon that threatens creative collaboration. The frail human mind can also throw a few psychological wrenches into the works. The mental pressure of "full creative disclosure" can intensify psychological dysfunctions and can even produce behavioral anomalies. (We all know people who were absolute sweethearts outside of band practice but became raving dictators once they touched an instrument.) Creation can be a brutal muse, and some people can't handle the price tag for inspiration. Compound all of this with the fact that collaboration often requires sharing your deepest passions with a committee, and you've got a recipe for mayhem.

One thing is for certain, some personalities *always* spell trouble. The first step toward constructive collaboration is recognizing any qualities in your creative partners that may endanger the project. Whether the talent of a dysfunctional collaborator merits tolerance is a personal choice. In any case, forewarned is forearmed. What follows is a rogues gallery of dangerous personalities.

The center-of-the-universe complex. An individual doesn't have to be an established superstar to tote around an enormous ego. Legions of ordinary people are often incredibly impressed with themselves, despite the fact they have accomplished absolutely nothing of significance. Go figure. Egotists are frustrating collaborators because they require constant attention, and they seldom listen unless you happen to be praising them. Such one-sided communication inhibits a free-flowing exchange of ideas.

Eggheads. Some people are literal thinkers. This type of mindset can be problematic when dealing with music because creativity doesn't always follow a straight path from A to B. Those who can't deal with the wild ride of conceptual whimsy often subvert creative collaboration by focusing on structural elements that they *can* understand.

For example, notation is music's universal language. However, music is not merely a collection of notes, chords, and rhythms on a staff; it requires "unnotated" elements such as passion and sensitivity to bring it to life. This is why an old Pablo Casals recording might move you to tears, but the identical piece performed by a younger, more technically adept cellist may not affect you at all. Now, if you handed a literal thinker a score with instructions to play the piece "with an almost unbearable sorrow," he or she would obsess over the rudiments of the song and disregard the work's emotional subtext. For many styles of music, such an approach is tantamount to murder.

Those who can't deal with the wild ride of conceptual whimsy often subvert creative collaboration by focusing on structural elements that they can understand.

Flakes. I've never met a flake who wasn't a nice person. They sincerely apologize when they forget rehearsals. They are sufficiently repentant when their tardiness causes a waiting producer to go ballistic. They're even truly embarrassed when they can't remember songs, lyrics, and chord changes. And when their foibles cause a project to self-destruct, they are usually very, very sorry.

Control freaks and musical popes. Collaboration is a process of give and take. Unfortunately, control freaks don't give much up. In a fierce effort to dominate a creative partnership, the control freak destroys the very essence of collaboration. But don't confuse the control freak with a strong leader. A sensitive creative director always seeks out the best idea because the quality of the work is all that matters. Control freaks, however, often champion the weaker idea simply because it is theirs.

Musical popes don't bother forcing their agendas on others because they practice creative infallibility. However, this pious attitude can be equally frustrating and detrimental to collaborative efforts. If the pope performs a piece in a musically or emotionally inappropriate manner, you're stuck. He or she will never change their part because the musical problem simply cannot be *their* fault.

12-step poster children. Despite the mythology surrounding tortured artists, severe addictions to drugs and/or alcohol seldom open the mind's eye to creative brilliance. The majority of addicts are simply befuddled wrecks. And disregarding your personal feel-ings about chemically controlled lifestyles, let's just deal with logistics. The addict/partner will rarely be where you need them when you need them, or in shape to do what you need them to do. You can't collaborate with a ghost.

Love bugs. If someone in your band is dating (or is married to) someone else in your band, you could be courting disaster. I'm sorry, but that's the way it is. It's incredibly difficult to be creatively and personally intimate with the same person. Some people pull it off, and I salute them. But why gamble with the two most important things in life: music and love?

PRODUCTIVITY INSURANCE

It is possible you'll encounter collaborators who possess no dysfunctions whatsoever, but you shouldn't bet on it. That doesn't mean that all collaborations are doomed. Combat-free collaboration is only possible when sticky issues are resolved early in the partnership. Collaborators should acknowledge their goals and needs, cop to their personal quirks, and specify responsibilities and rewards. Put everything on the table. If you can't deal comfortably with business issues, you'll probably experience difficulty collaborating on creative projects. Follow your gut: if you feel uneasy about something, bail out. However, if you're loathe to trust premonitions, here are some practical tips for avoiding creative conflicts.

Embrace your dysfunctions. Just admit it. We all possess traits that can sabotage collaboration. Artists who understand the less-

*A declaration of purpose ensures
that everyone knows what is going on
from day one.*

productive aspects of their psyches can compensate for behavioral land mines. In addition, conceding that you're as bonkers as your creative partners increases tolerance levels. The more collaborators understand each other, the better the chance for success.

Define the project. I don't know why it's so hard for artists to define what they're doing and why. The amount of serious projects that begin without a game plan is staggering. Vague alliances can be big trouble when collaborators discover they're in a project for different reasons.

You can avoid future tensions by having the creative partners approve a simple statement of purpose. Write down the partnership's goals—"We're collaborating on a song to be shopped to music publishers"; "We're forming a band to play local clubs"; "We're forming a commercial pop band for the express purpose of seeking a major-label record deal"; and so on—and have everyone involved sign the document. This agreement is not a legal contract, just a reality check. A declaration of purpose ensures that everyone knows what is going on from day one. Consider it your first collaboration.

Clarify responsibilities. As equally important as defining a project is deciding who does what. Every project generates tons of practical questions that must be answered to ensure smooth operation. Is there a band leader? Who contacts the music industry? Who books the clubs? Who keeps the books? The list of administrative chores is endless. It's essential that all partners understand what is expected of them. Otherwise, you'll be fighting over who forgot to mail the demo to the big-name producer who needed your song for an album project. The joy of blaming someone else for screwing up will not ease the pain of a blown opportunity.

Determine the rewards. Sometimes the music industry seems like one big arena full of artists fighting over profit participation. You know the drill: Two people write a song or produce a record, and the project rockets up the charts. The royalties start gushing and suddenly someone isn't getting what they consider a fair share. Say hello to months or years of legal trench warfare. No wonder many musicians and songwriters are petrified of collaboration; they're afraid of being ripped off.

Such fear should be unwarranted. Before you begin your collaboration, write up a simple agreement that lays out the division of the profit percentages of the work in question. Then, agree that some percentages may be amended to more accurately reflect contributions to the final product. This two-step process may seem like one step too many, but it's essential to deal with revenue issues early in the creative process.

When the project is completed, review the agreement and make sure all collaborators confirm and accept their "shares" before filing copyright forms and other business and legal documents. Also, don't forget to determine who owns the store—the master tape, composition copyright, band name, etc.—before

It's certainly a fair exchange if a few arguments and misunderstandings occur along the way to a brilliant collective effort.

signing any pertinent legal agreements.

Count to ten. If you lose your temper, you also lose the argument. This means that you can't critically assess a situation if you're out of control. In addition, an aggressive posture can make collaborators defensive, and soon everyone is too busy screaming to do any listening.

No matter how much you want to throttle a pompous ass, remember that a calm demeanor is infinitely more productive than a temper tantrum. Channeling for inspiration—or devising brilliant solutions to creative problems—is difficult when all you want to do is tear someone's head off. So if things heat up between you and your partner, step back, take a breath, count to ten, then continue the discussion. If necessary, tell your collaborator that you're just too angry to discuss the situation rationally and propose that you take a break from each other for however long seems right (a few minutes, an hour, etc.).

SURVIVOR'S CLUB

Collaboration tends to bring out the best *and* worst in people. But despite the risks, a wonderful dynamic occurs when the right bunch of people pour their creative juices into a melting pot. Although negotiating the ebb and flow of multiple creative energies can be fatiguing, the results are usually worth the struggle.

It's certainly a fair exchange if a few arguments and misunderstandings occur along the way to a brilliant collective effort. Devotion to the project at hand is paramount, and this allegiance is also the final safeguard for effective collaboration. If anyone—or anything—threatens the artistic health of a project, terminate the troublemaker with extreme prejudice. And that's the *only* combat tactic sensible collaborators should initiate.

CHAPTER 2

Hiring an Engineer

Making music is extremely personal, and home recordists—by virtue of their comfortable isolation—are perhaps the most guarded at inviting outsiders into their creative spaces. But if the goal of all your creative efforts is producing a brilliant master tape, judicious use of outside professionals makes perfect sense. If your music is important to you, you owe it to yourself to make the best tape possible. Don't let fear or egotism brand your beautiful song with a distorted vocal track or a muddy mix.

A poorly recorded or mixed tape devalues your work. If you're not a great mixer or you have difficulty recording vocals and other acoustic instruments, don't settle for mediocre masters. And as the audio industry continues to produce affordable, master-quality tools for the home recordist, how well those tools are used becomes critical. Some artists have the engineering chops to release commercial products from their bedrooms, while most others may need a little help. The latter group can always hire a professional recording engineer to spice up their home recordings.

Most recording engineers are fanatics. If given carte blanche to schedule sessions, they'd devour an entire month auditioning microphones and mic placement for each instrument. Then, they'd spend the rest of the year refining gain stages, tweaking EQ, and programming signal processors. A deadline is often the only reason that a project gets completed at all. And during those rare moments when an engineer isn't in the studio, he or she is usually studying new records for interesting sounds, checking out the latest audio gear, or reading trade magazines. But devotion to excellence isn't the only reason engineers are so driven. Survival is paramount. If a pro engineer *doesn't* get great sounds, he or she doesn't work. Period.

Like I said earlier, pro engineers are not the only people capable of recording great tracks. I've heard some amazing home demos that absolutely shamed tracks recorded in big, expensive studios. But if you're looking for consistently high-quality tracks, the law of averages is on the side of those who make their living honing their skills. And anyway, artists are usually more interested in documenting ideas and performances than sweating over the timbral nuances of a vocal track or other sound source. So, even if you do have decent engineering chops, perhaps you're better off allowing yourself to focus on your craft, leaving the technical details to the pros.

ENGINEERING HELP

A good engineer can step into any recording environment and deliver the goods. This talent is a boon to home recordists, who should consider hiring a pro engineer whenever a critical phase of a project lies beyond their expertise or competence. For example, most musicians can deal with MIDI tracks just fine, but recording a clean vocal is often a hit-or-

Even if you do have decent engineering chops, perhaps you're better off allowing yourself to focus on your craft, leaving the technical details to the pros.

miss proposition. Poor vocal recordings can be caused by inexperience and sometimes by lack of proper microphones. Because most independent engineers own a collection of good mics, the home recordist can take advantage of the pro's chops *and* equipment.

Mixing is another area were many artists fall down. The tracks may have been well recorded, but the "final assembly" ends up muddy, over-processed, and/or noisy. Engineers specializing in mixdowns are legion, and you owe it to yourself to ensure that your final product sounds as good as possible.

In addition, as the line between pro and home studios blurs, hybrid projects offer artists the best of both worlds. For instance, you could flesh out a song on a home MIDI system, mix a stereo reference track (and time code, if necessary) to a hard-disk recorder or MDM, and take the tape to a pro studio to record live drums. Back at home, you can agonize over vocals, then hire a mixing specialist to come over and mix your masterpiece.

Finding an engineer is easy. Call some local recording studios and inquire if their staff engineers are available for outside work. If not, many studio managers have lists of reputable independent (freelance) engineers. Local bands that have recently completed recording projects are also good sources for referrals. Ask them if they liked working with a certain engineer and get his or her telephone number. Usually the local musician's grapevine is filled with informa-

tion on hot engineers. Finally, commercial listings are available for just about every metropolitan area.

Most engineers charge an hourly rate for their services, although project fees (one lump sum for the life of the project) are sometimes negotiable. Happily, rates are usually negotiable. On the other extreme, remix engineers with successful track records don't bargain very much.

THE AUDITIONS

An empathetic working relationship is essential to musician/engineer collaborations, as the engineer must translate your ideas into sound. To ensure harmony throughout a project—and a final master that meets, or hopefully exceeds, your expectations—a face-to-face meeting is critical.

Play some examples of your work, detail your influences, and discuss how you envision the project's sound. Bring examples of CDs that you like. If the engineer turns white, giggles, or sneers as you play your favorite recording, he or she probably isn't right for your project. If you plan to hire the engineer to work in your home studio, make sure that you trust them. Don't be afraid to ask for project credits, and be sure to contact everyone the engineer cites as a reference.

It's extremely helpful to provide an independent engineer with a complete list of your equipment. During the session, they may be able to optimize your setup with a personal

*If you feel your tracks have been
poorly recorded, get a second opinion from
a reputable recording studio.*

processing rack or better mics. Be sure to ask if they charge extra for providing their own equipment. In addition, apprise the engineer of any outside noise problems (crying babies in the next apartment, etc.), time limitations, and equipment quirks (the mute on channel seven is intermittent, and so on). Providing such information is more than just common courtesy, it ensures the engineer can do the best job possible.

BAD SEEDS

If you're past the age of five, you've probably figured out that life is seldom fair. This discovery triggers countless moral dilemmas throughout one's life, but the one we're concerned with here is why bad engineers get gigs. Unfortunately, there are no easy answers to that one.

These bad seeds inflict tracks with everything from savagely distorted signals to ground-loop hums. A story circulated about one engineer in the San Francisco area who was notorious for falling asleep during sessions. On one occasion, a vocalist finished an impassioned vocal performance and heard snoring in his headphones. Puzzled, he walked out of the vocal booth to find the engineer face down on the mixing board. Unfortunately, sleeping beauty had landed on the talkback mic and slate buttons. As a result, the snoring was recorded to tape along with the vocal. Scratch one brilliant vocal track. The really depressing punch line is that this indi-vidual was able to run a successful studio for years.

But who keeps these bad seeds working? We do! If you have a terrible experience with an engineer be sure to spread the word. Do not recommend engineers who do bad work, have bad habits, or are otherwise unprofessional. Don't be sheepish! If you feel your tracks have been poorly recorded, get a second opinion from a reputable recording studio. Some studio managers will put up your tape and check it out at no charge, as long as it's during studio downtime or a session break. No one likes to have shoddy engineers waltzing around, taking hard-earned money and churning out crap. Bad seeds soil the reputations of every hard-working engineer and recording studio.

Unfortunately, it's practically impossible to get your money back from an unprofessional independent engineer. Because they're freelance, they answer to nobody. (Recording studios, like most reputable businesses, usually make good on their mistakes.) A butchered master tape is often one of those painful "live and learn" experiences. The only solution is to find a *reputable* engineer and retrack or remix the project as needed.

CHAPTER 3

Hiring a Producer

istory has proven that when a passionate and committed artist is matched with an empathetic producer, the world is treated to the likes of the Beatles and George Martin or Michael Jackson and Quincy Jones.

At best, a good producer can help you more fully interpret your artistry and harness your creativity into succinct musical statements. He or she may also have the commercial savvy to guide you toward a hit record. But even if the relationship doesn't produce an artistic epiphany or a smash hit, the presence of an objective critic can force you to respect and hone your craft. That's not exactly a small gift.

Unfortunately, because some artists believe they surrender total creative control when they hire a producer, the process of finding a suitable collaborator can be stressful. Much of this discomfort revolves around less-than-accurate preconceptions of the producer's role in music making.

THE PRODUCER MYTH

Many musicians assume that producers are musical despots who view artists as merely the clay for their sonic sculpturing. Some producers *do* fit this description, and there's a sure-fire way to avoid falling into their clutches: Don't hire them! Most producers, however, are sensitive and caring collaborators who don't deserve your apprehensions or paranoia. Good producers, like film directors,

draw the best performances from talented artists and ensure that the project maintains some level of conceptual cohesiveness.

Many producers also help with administrative functions so the artist can focus exclusively on creative matters. They will book the recording studio; hire the engineer and any necessary session musicians; develop and maintain a tracking schedule; administer the recording budget; and oversee mastering and duplication. But a producer's main responsibility is as vague as it is simple: to make a good recording.

PRODUCER'S PREROGATIVES

How a producer "makes a good recording" can take many directions. Following are three main production methods. These overviews are offered to provide a general understanding of the producer's craft and are far from comprehensive. In addition, many producers combine elements of all three methods.

Producers often choose their production methodology based on their view of your current artistic sophistication, the strength of your material, and your overall personality. It's imperative that musicians also take some responsibility for forming the artist/producer relationship. Use the following definitions to decide how *you* want to work. Be honest about how much—or how little—production assistance you need.

Documentation. Alternative music recordist Steve Albini (Nirvana, P.J. Harvey, and

Good producers, like film directors, draw the best performances from talented artists and ensure that the project maintains some level of conceptual cohesiveness.

others) hates being called a producer. Albini believes that you should stay out of a band's way; simply record the musicians live, documenting their creativity in its purest form. For some artists, this approach can be quite liberating. So why hire such a producer, if they only capture what you've already got?

Even documentary recordings need an outside ear to evaluate the quality and intensity of the tracks. Artists shouldn't have to worry about how they sound; they should be free to concentrate on delivering an evocative performance. And if you still don't think that a "documentation" producer is earning his or her paycheck, keep in mind that it's not an easy task identifying the minute nuances that make one performance better than another. Try it sometime.

Music editing. Some artists need a little more help to realize their creative potential. A producer may decide to "edit" their work, much like a copy editor proofs a literary manuscript. For example, if the song lyrics are inconsistent, the producer may request revisions (or attempt to personally rewrite problem lines). Or if the musical arrangement has a lot of "fat," the producer will suggest deleting sections that seem superfluous or overly repetitive.

In addition, the producer monitors the performance to ensure that the artist isn't over-reaching his or her ability. Many vocalists, for instance, insist on singing in keys that are beyond a comfortable vocal range. A good producer makes sure that whatever remains

on tape or hard disk is the best representation of the artist's talent.

The svengali. Sometimes an artist may have personal charisma and an interesting "sound" but limited facility for musical communication. In these instances, a producer may write the songs (or find suitable freelance songwriters), form a support band for the artist, and choose a musical direction. This method is more prevalent in pop music and is often vilified by critics.

Criticism aside, this approach is more widespread than fans may realize. Vocalists such as Joe Cocker, Mariah Carey, Michael Bolton, and Whitney Houston seldom write their own material and are certainly counseled on musical direction and delivery by their respective producers. I don't believe the more "hands-on" approach of these producers diminishes the talent of their clients. Many fans would hate to be cheated from enjoying Houston's incredible voice just because she doesn't write her hits.

AUDITION TIME

Now that you have a basic idea about how producers work, how do you find the person that's right for your project? It's unfair to judge producers by specific projects because the projects often transcend stylistic genres. A producer may work with rap artists, rock bands, and new age instrumentalists, making great records with each. Of course, there's also the tenet that unless you're immersed in

*If you do get nervous about
contractual matters, see a lawyer before
you sign anything.*

a musical style, you can't do it justice. Are we confused, yet?

It is difficult to audition a producer based solely on his or her demo reel. Just because someone specializes in rap music doesn't mean they would automatically be a bad match for a pop band. Sometimes the cross-pollination of musical styles produces interesting and wonderful results. Because of this, consider the demo reel as a preliminary measure of professional competence. Forget the musical style for a moment. Does the song sound professional? Would it stand up to what you hear on the radio and MTV? Did the producer allow obvious mistakes or poor performances to stand? Is the song well arranged? How creatively did the producer deal with the sonic spectrum and subject matter? Do you like what you hear?

If the demo reel shows the producer to be competent, then you can get down to the nitty-gritty. Schedule a meeting to discuss your artistic goals. Talk about artists that you respect and records that you love. Don't forget to voice your career goals: is the project designed to acquire a major-label recording contract, or do you have other plans? The available recording budget should also be discussed. The more the producer knows about you and your music, the better. Remember, you're forging a creative alliance, so make sure both parties know exactly what they're getting into.

After all is said and done, ask yourself whether you trust this person. Do you believe

that he or she has the necessary chops to take your artistic vision to a higher level? Are you comfortable with this person making brutal assessments and criticisms of your work? If you answer "no" to any of these questions, don't hire the producer in question. If you're uncomfortable now, you'll *really* be in ulcerville halfway through the recording sessions. Don't set yourself up for a fall. Wait until you find a producer that you feel good about.

PAY SCALES

Most mid-level producers charge an hourly or project rate for their services (also refered to as a "per side" rate, meaning per song), and the rate varies depending on how much they contribute to the project. They may also ask for a percentage of *your* record-company advance, if the demo they produce gets you a deal. This figure is typically three to five percent of the gross advance payment. In all cases, be sure to get the particulars in writing. A lawyer might be unnecessary, unless you're going for the big deal, but a typed agreement letter is essential. Have both parties—artist and producer—agree to the terms and sign the document.

A production agreement doesn't have to be a scary thing. It's simply a tangible document that spells out the responsibilities of a creative collaboration. Specify what the producer is doing (producing two songs, remixing one track, and so on), and how much they are getting paid for their services. If down-

A production agreement doesn't have to be a scary thing. It's simply a tangible document that spells out the responsibilities of a creative collaboration.

stream percentages are promised, put them in writing. For example, state that the producer will receive 2.5 percent of the gross record-company advance should the producer's work be responsible for sealing the record deal. (It should be no secret if the demo in question catches the ears of the industry.) And if you *do* get nervous about these contractual matters, see a lawyer before you sign anything.

CHAPTER 4

Personal Managers

Although a personal manager may be the critical factor in an act's success, surprisingly few musicians really know what a manager does. There's a reason why so many artists—whose careers may ultimately depend on the business acumen of a savvy manager—are ignorant to the whys and wherefores of artist management. That's because managers do most of their work *behind* the scenes.

Chances are, you'll never even hear about an artist's manager unless you read the music trades or some juicy scandal erupts. Most managers try to get publicity for their clients, rather than themselves, so it's easy to see why a number of myths and misconceptions about personal managers have developed.

WHAT MANAGERS DO

A manager's primary objective is to advance his or her client's career. During an artist's development phase, that objective often means providing constructive criticism and mapping out a career strategy. A good manager-artist team works together to set realistic goals and ensure that songwriting, image presentation, and other creative and marketing factors are as strong as they can be. Personal managers should not be confused with business managers whose task it is to handle the financial aspects of an artist's career. With that distinction out of the way, and for the sake of this discussion, we'll refer to personal managers simply as managers.

A manager's first task is to generate interest in the act. There's not much money to deal with when the act isn't making any. At this point in the relationship, the manager will begin getting the word out through press releases, word of mouth, and so on. Managers also work to set their clients apart from the crowd. And even though artists usually define their own images, the manager can certainly help refine that image until it is something fresh and unique.

Few artists can hope to score a label or publishing deal without representation. And because of the huge investment needed to develop successful recording acts, labels typically deal only with industry veterans who have proven track records. An unrepresented artist seeking his or her first record contract is hardly an attractive prospect. A reputable manager who has handled or "discovered" commercial talent, however, can get a demo played for the right ears. Unlike artists, who always think they deserve a deal, a manager won't waste an executive's time with an act that's subpar or not yet ready for the market.

Smart managers often increase their clout by entering a relationship with a heavyweight music lawyer or agent. If that person has enough industry connections and power to seal a deal, the manager may even step aside and let him or her handle the actual pitch. All-in-all, a manager's talent for assembling a team of powerful and influential people to champion an artist is often the critical factor in seducing record labels.

Many managers aren't interested in working with artists that don't have a short- or long-term vision for their success.

Finally, a good manager strives to save artists from themselves. Too often, an artist falls victim to a terminal case of self-importance, which can result in tragic creative decisions. In these instances, the manager should be an objective and trusted advisor, who always tries to steer the artist back to the agreed-upon career path.

DEAL-MAKING MACHINERY

The counsel of a strong, savvy manager is critical when an artist is ready to sign his or her first record contract. Too often, the excitement of an impending deal overwhelms an artist's business sense, which can make contract negotiations a dangerous game. This is where the manager's role as advisor comes into play: part of the manager's job is to help their client make sound decisions.

Obviously, getting the artist signed is only half the battle. The manager must ensure that a label is solidly behind the act, otherwise the artist will never get the exposure necessary to build a fan base. Some of the things managers push for on behalf of their clients are adequate recording budgets and money to promote the act; they also make sure that the label execs don't forget about their clients, otherwise the project will get lost among the 50 other acts the exec has on his or her plate.

A manager's job doesn't end there, either. They also coordinate the other members of the artist's team, including the lawyer, accountant, booking agent, road manager, and business manager. In addition, they must interface with all the label personnel working the act, such as A&R executives, promotional reps, and the business affairs staff.

ARE YOU READY?

Having a manager sounds like a pretty good deal, doesn't it? It's nice to have someone handling all the business aspects of your career while you concentrate solely on being an *artiste*. However, if your creativity isn't producing any revenues, you'll find it very difficult to convince a reputable manager to work with you.

One mistake artists make is looking for management too early in their careers. In general, if you can do it yourself, you should do it yourself. Some musicians may refute this advice, believing that their obvious talent should be enticement enough for a manager. These artists should take a hard look at where they stand in the industry. If you're consistently playing to the bartender and six disinterested winos at trashy clubs and can't even get it together to record a demo, face it, you're probably not ready for a manager.

Look at your career from the manager's perspective. Before managers commit their resources to develop acts, they must believe there's a chance at some kind of return. No one would undertake the constant, crippling headaches of artist management if there weren't the prospect of a big payday. Even in best-case scenarios where an artist does possess commercial talent, there's no guarantee

Unlike artists, who always think they deserve a deal, a manager won't waste an executive's time with an act that's subpar or not yet ready for the market.

they'll find a large public and sell massive amounts of records. Some managers understandably hedge their bets by seeking out clients who are already generating some interest from record labels. At the very least, you should have a strong regional following and enough material to put out at least one album. This way, you'll be more attractive to a manager and can at least give him or her something to work with.

Unfortunately, not every band starts its career with an industry buzz. The Beatles were turned down by just about every label in England before that fateful meeting with George Martin at EMI Records—a meeting that was arranged by the band's manager, Brian Epstein.

HAPPY TOGETHER

The artist-manager relationship is an extremely close one. Therefore, it's critical that the parties involved are compatible. Forging a long, successful alliance with a manager requires starting off on the right foot. Be sure to quiz potential managers on their industry clout, past and current successes, and musical tastes.

Don't be afraid to ask about the manager's connections with the industry, and how he or she would go about representing the band to labels. Ask what the manager would do first: shop a demo, book showcases, or help develop the act. You should also get the manager's take on the band's potential and the day-to-day protocol he or she follows when working with artists.

Successful creative relationships require vision, so test the manager's strategic chops by asking for a tentative long-term plan. The manager should be able to articulate where he or she sees you in one year and again in five years. You should also have thought out your own long-term plan. Many managers aren't interested in working with artists that don't have a short- or long-term vision for their success. The manager-artist relationship is far from one-sided. Managers also have career concerns, and they seek out artists who have the drive to succeed.

THE CONTRACT QUESTION

We've already established that managers don't work for free. However, there is no industry standard for what they do get. Generally, management fees run between fifteen and twenty percent of the artist's *gross* income.

Often, established artists pay their managers fifteen percent and their booking agent ten percent. But if a band is new and they know the manager isn't going to see any money at the front-end of the relationship, they might be inclined to give the manager a higher commission for a specified period to shop a record deal, find an agent, and so on—basically get the act established.

The revenue streams on which management commissions are based are not necessarily limited to record sales and live gigs: everything is negotiable. In general, management fees are based on everything that the

The best managers are extremely busy,
but they're also on the look-out for
future prospects.

artist does in the entertainment industry. That includes commercial endorsements, music publishing, producing royalties, film contracts, and other creative properties.

As for management contracts, most lawyers advise getting everything in writing. However, some managers are comfortable working with verbal agreements. Technically, a verbal agreement is as legally binding as a written one, although if a dispute arises, the terms of a verbal agreement can be difficult to verify. Some personal managers and artists choose to work together for a while before they mutually decide to put something in writing—sort of a test-drive period for both parties.

However, almost all managers agree that a written contract—to protect both parties— is extremely important once a record deal is on the table. Every contract is different, but the typical agreement covers five years. Some carry a clause that terminates the contract if specified revenue projections are not achieved. Other contracts might cover only a single project, or span a two- or three-record deal, with options available to extend the relationship. It's important to remember that most contracts can be broken or renegotiated, although it could be costly, depending on the circumstance.

CLOSING THE DEAL

So, if you have trouble getting the attention of a desired manager, be gently persistent. The best managers are extremely busy, but they're also on the look-out for future prospects. Don't give up. Invite the manager to your gigs, and be sure to keep him or her on your mailing list until you establish a connection.

When you do enter a relationship with a manager, hopefully it will be a union of mutual respect and honest friendship. However, a trustworthy and loyal alliance doesn't mean that you should abdicate personal accountability for your business affairs. Remember, the more responsible you are earlier in your career, the more money you'll have later in your career.

CHAPTER 5

Entertainment Lawyers

The role of attorneys in the music industry has expanded considerably in recent years. They do everything from negotiating deals to running labels to litigating courtroom fights on behalf of battling band members. And because of these wide-ranging roles, they have had an increasing impact in shaping the industry.

Basically, entertainment lawyers are general practitioners with a specialized type of clientele: the working musician. Any lawyer representing musicians must have a working knowledge of intellectual property rights, which is a musician's most valuable asset. This area of legal expertise includes copyright law (protecting songs and recordings), trademark law (protecting the group names and logos used by musicians), and with today's fast-moving technological landscape, patent law (protecting new technology and/or ideas of the musician).

Because the protection and exploitation of this intellectual property requires that the musician deal with third parties such as record companies, publishing companies, managers, and other musicians, most entertainment lawyers develop their expertise in the field of contract law. Entertainment lawyers also help their clients with issues involving the establishment of businesses. These issues include legal formation of a business, licensing, taxes, and so on.

LESS OBVIOUS ROLES

An attorney can be a great asset during the early stages of a musician's career. For example, lawyers are often called upon to shop demos on behalf of clients. Many record labels and publishers are unwilling to accept demos unless they are solicited or forwarded to them by a lawyer. (These labels like to be assured that an artist or writer has been legally advised before sending off their wares.)

A lawyer can also fill the role of personal manager and general "trusted industry advisor." As you work to define either of these roles with a lawyer, be aware of the boundaries each of you are setting and what the compensation should be for services above and beyond standard legal assistance.

THE RIGHT MATCH

As you can surmise, law practices that service the needs of musicians can range from solo practitioners in tiny offices to huge firms renting out entire floors of office buildings. Some companies are large enough to justify having in-house counsel. (Many major record labels, such as Sony or Warner Bros., have entire staffs of lawyers working for them.) Choosing the right attorney can be as difficult as finding the right drummer for your band, but it doesn't have to be a daunting effort if you do your homework. As with a search for a drummer, I suggest you look for

It is important to establish with the lawyer the scope of the services to be rendered and how you will be billed for them.

a combination of skill, reputation, and desire, and don't discount the importance of compatibility or your "gut instinct."

Prior to an initial consultation, find out as much as you can about the lawyer you're considering. Researching bar associations and professional organizations, reading articles and/or books published by the lawyer, and even attending a seminar or class where you can see the lawyer in action are all good ways to investigate a lawyer's work. The *Yellow Pages* is certainly a source for names, as well, but be advised that anyone can purchase a cool ad saying they practice entertainment law. As with anything else in the industry, the best source for your search is to ask around in the music community. Ask other acts and individuals you meet for referrals, and get their opinions on the lawyer's style, professionalism, and fees. Remember to temper the comments with the client's results; many times artists will blame a bad deal on the lawyer who negotiated the deal. In many such cases, there was nothing the lawyer could do to rectify a bad bargaining position.

The initial meeting is your opportunity to get that valuable first impression. Use this time to be succinct about your expectations and to see whether you anticipate a personality conflict. Some lawyers use an initial consultation first meeting as a chance to learn something about your long- and short-term goals, seriousness, and business savvy. Many times, these lawyers will either conduct the initial interview for no fee or for a reduced

fee. Other lawyers make it clear up front that every second spent with you—including listening to your case and getting to know you—is billable.

CAVEAT EMPTOR

Repeat this phrase three times before you read any further: Time is money. An entertainment lawyer's fees vary as much as the cost of hiring a musician or producer to do a recording session for you. Both a lawyer's and a musician's fees are based largely on skill, reputation, and demand for their time. The three common ways lawyers charge for their services are hourly, on a percentage basis, or on a retainer basis.

The simplest way to pay for a lawyer is by the hour. Hourly rates can range from $100 to $500, including telephone time, reviewing or drafting contracts, attending meetings on your behalf, court time, etc. Although this fee can end up being in the thousands of dollars for certain services, the firm will usually be flexible regarding payment, either arranging for payment over time or providing the service in stages so you can control how far you wish to go into a project without getting in over your head financially. For example, in an attempt to collect back royalties owed to you, a demand letter would be one stage of fees, negotiating a settlement the next, and a full-blown lawsuit the final stage.

Hiring a firm on retainer means paying a set negotiated fee for all services required by

Repeat this phrase three times
before you read any further:
Time is money.

you, which is usually calculated on a monthly basis. It is much like having a session player "on call" for your studio projects. Some months the lawyer will be extremely busy, other months will be very slow. Usually, a retainer is not negotiated between attorney and client until a working relationship and idea of work flow is established.

The final version of fee structure is the percentage or "spec" (short for speculative) basis. In these types of arrangements, the lawyer performs legal services in exchange for a percentage of some facet of your career. For example, the lawyer will negotiate your record deal for a percentage of the deal. Before you decide to enter into this kind of agreement and celebrate getting "something for nothing," take a step back to think about this for a moment. One of a lawyer's primary services and obligations to you is to advise you of deals or certain terms of your contract that are not in your best interest. I am not implying that lawyers working on a percentage have a conflict of interest, but remember that if the lawyer's entire fee is based on (1) your signing a deal and (2) how much of an advance you will be getting up front (an advance, by the way, that you will be paying back from royalties), it may reduce the likelihood that you will be advised to turn down a deal if it's the only one on the table.

It is important to establish with the lawyer the scope of the services to be rendered and how you will be billed for them. Many times, hybrids (e.g., part hourly, part

spec, or spec with a cap on fees) are structured between the parties. Be sure that the understanding is expressed in a written agreement. If fees are a pressing issue, try to find volunteer or low-fee lawyers providing legal services for artists. Check your local telephone listings for these services.

In the event that you have a disagreement with your lawyer and feel that a legitimate issue exists, you can file a complaint against the lawyer in question with your state's bar association. Prior to doing this, it is important that you evaluate whether the issue is between you and your lawyer or between you and the party with whom you and your lawyer are dealing. If a referral service provided you with the lawyer, it is important that you notify them of any problems you have, as well.

ERGO

Given the nature of the entertainment industry, lawyers and their clout rise with the success of their clients. Remember that hiring a law firm with major clients does not make your tape sound any better or automatically make you any more knowledgeable about the business. You will be doing yourself and your lawyer a great service by familiarizing yourself with your business dealings and by having an open enough dialog with your lawyer to let him or her act on your behalf.

2

Taking It to the Street

The Secrets to Networking, Promoting, and Gigging Your Way to Success

CHAPTER 6

Do You Have What It Takes to Get Signed?

One truth should be clear to you by now: The music industry is a risky business for everyone involved. And no place is this more evident than in the signing of a new act to a record contract. The label is risking its reputation and resources on an unproven artist, and the artist is putting his or career into someone else's hands. However, the more savvy you are at delivering what the labels are looking for, the better your chances of success.

THE ACT

Obviously, without an act, there's no record deal. Most labels look for something that sets an artist apart from the crowd. This "something" can be as simple as a singer/songwriter who can sing and write incredibly well or an act that is breaking new ground in visual presentation. The artist that exhibits a strong identity or possesses an engaging artistic vision has the best chances of igniting public interest.

But no matter how great the artistic vision, there is absolutely no substitute for talent. Musicians often groan and cite no-talents who made it solely because of "connections," but the truth is that long-term success in the record industry is earned by innate talent, rehearsal, hard work, and production chops. The experience gained by paying dues in clubs and recording studios is immeasurable.

THE PRODUCT

The music—or "product" as it's known in the industry—is the most important component of a record deal. It is terribly difficult to attract the ears of major-label executives without good songs. Your repertoire doesn't have to include formulaic copies of hit songs, but you should objectively evaluate whether the material will reach a broad audience within your musical genre.

After all, going into a pro studio and hiring a producer to make a full-blown demo is a major financial commitment. Make sure that your songs and act are developed enough to warrant the expense. Many groups maximize their recording investment by pressing their own CDs and selling them at gigs. Taking the DIY route is a big commitment, but it can reap career rewards. Ani DiFranco has enjoyed great success without a major label behind her, and the artist formerly known as Prince retreated from the major-label scene and now enjoys complete control of his career (and his song royalties). Even if you don't want to be a DIYer for your entire career, it never hurts to prove to labels that your act has commercial possibilities by selling enough self-produced CDs to become a regional success. In fact, so many artists are enjoying success on their own or on independent labels, that major labels consider the indie route to be a sort of record industry "minor league" proving ground.

Today, many artists are stretching beyond

It is terribly difficult to attract
the ears of major-label executives
without good songs.

the basic audio demo. A presentation that transcends a mere collection of songs can really pay-off, especially in the current wave of video games and multimedia presentations. If your group is terrific live, a live showcase or concert videotape can be more effective than an audio-only demo. CD-ROM demos are an interesting, hi-tech way to showcase both your band and your marketing savvy. And having a Web site with audio and video clips of your act is a convenient and hip way to show off your talents.

Occasionally, there's the happily-ever-after scenario in which very basic demos or no demos at all got an act signed. Unfortunately, the industry *is* spoiled by great sounding master tapes and exciting videos. You need to evaluate how much latitude your budget allows, and to paraphrase the Bard, the song is the thing. Given the choice between spending your money on a master-quality demo or an amateurish one packaged with a lame video, choose the killer audio demo. A demo that truly represents your sound is more beneficial than a poorly realized video or CD-ROM product.

THE BUZZ

Call it "press," "the local buzz," or "unabashed self-promotion," but any media attention an act can generate will boost its chances of getting a deal. Publicity, in the form of concert or demo/record reviews, interviews, and "gossip" pieces, creates great name recognition. If

the same act keeps popping up as "a name everyone is talking about," labels take notice.

Media manipulation is often the most important promotional tool for selling a record. An act that can make the shift from persons to *personalities* and deliver great interviews is very attractive to labels. When preparing for a record release or small tour, it makes good business sense to put energy into self-promotion. If you don't have the time or the skills to deal with the media, hire a publicist to coordinate press relations.

THE TEAM

Finding and building a team to help shop and hammer out a deal is crucial to your success. These are the people who will help you identify your talents, vision, and commercial worth. They will also seek the handful of label executives high enough in the industry food chain to make real decisions about your act. And when it comes time to negotiate the deal, the team will strive to ensure a good, honest evaluation of the relationship by both artist and label.

This coveted inner circle of advisors may consist of a personal manager, an agent, an entertainment lawyer, and a variety of industry contacts. Industry contacts typically include club owners, recording studio managers, performing rights society representatives, and record company employees. It should be no surprise that many of these people are trying to make it in the industry by

Call it "press," "the local buzz," or "unabashed self-promotion," but any media attention an act can generate will boost its chances of getting a deal.

finding "the next big thing," so their interest can be extremely beneficial. Some will stop at nothing to secure your act a deal because your success is also their success. If you happen to be buddies with a signed act, be sure to ask about the people that helped them get their deal. We're talking about serious networking, here. The more industry people you know, the more industry access you'll have.

When building your team, clearly define each member's role. Squabbles down the road—when a deal is being negotiated or has already been signed—can turn into ugly lawsuits if a team member feels they aren't being adequately compensated for their contribution. Work out all the "what if" scenarios before anyone takes a demo into a label office. It usually is smart business to compose a basic written agreement outlining who owns what, who gets what, and who controls whom. If you even think a relationship may get complicated, consult a lawyer.

Lastly, remember the earlier caveat about taking risks. The team shopping your wares is putting its reputation on the line. As an artist, you are also taking a risk by putting your career into their hands. Both parties should understand and agree about exactly what is expected of them. So, if you're looking for major-label riches, you need to do your part by honing your skills and assembling a reliable team. In short, you can make yourself a hot prospect by making yourself a low-risk investment.

CHAPTER 7

Seductive Promotion

In this age of e-mail, Web sites, and information that travels at the blink of an eye, it's encouraging to know that some things are best done the old-fashioned way. The traditional music promotional package is one such animal. Sure, you could establish a Web page with music and video clips of your band, but you still need to let people know where to find it. By sending out press kits, you not only inform the media and music industry execs of your band's existence, you deliver your music directly into their hands.

It never ceases to amaze me that otherwise gifted, intelligent artists can royally screw up something as simple as a promo kit. The contents are basic: a CD or CD-R, a press release about the current album, biographical information on the band, a photograph, contact information, and any pertinent press clippings. The challenge is that each of these components must be well crafted in order to generate any interest. It's not trivial, but if it were, I wouldn't be dedicating a whole chapter to it. Remember that your press kit is your introduction to industry pros, and to paraphrase an old shampoo ad, you only get one chance to make a first impression.

THE DATA GAME

The purpose of a promo package is to disseminate a band's music and background information in hopes of garnering radio airplay, reviews, or other industry interest. Many artists make the mistake of trying to be too cute or too clever with their press kits. It's true that creating a unique and unusual package will get you noticed; just make sure you're getting noticed in a *good* way. Industry pros have to deal with scads of CDs every day, so if they have to spend too much time trying to decipher a cryptic type style or layout, they might put off checking it out, or maybe they will forget altogether. Yes, they might be bypassing some good music, but it's your job to make them want to listen to it. They just want to be able to check out the information they need as quickly and easily as possible.

If you've never created a press kit before, your interests are best served by sticking to the basics. When it comes to your photo, the 8 x 10 black-and-white glossy is still the standard, as it reproduces the best in newspapers and magazines, but it's fine to send color if you prefer. Your press release, biographical information, and cover letter should be one page each. If you choose to include any press clippings, only send a few recent samples. A press kit the length of *War and Peace* will only incur the disdain of the recipient.

Simplicity is also the key when composing the copy for your press kit. Most people won't be interested in reading about every band you've performed with, unless, of course, you have played with artists of note. The data in your bio should be relevant to your musical talents and influences. For instance, include information about where your band is based, who does most of the music and lyric writing,

Let's not forget the most important element: the music itself. Always send out the best quality product you can afford.

who plays which instruments, and the evolution of your playing style. Don't just give a dull laundry list of facts; work hard at writing this information in an engaging manner. Basic does not mean boring. And even though I've emphasized keeping things simple, be sure to include any interesting anecdotes about how your band met, the recording of the album, and so on.

RELEASE ME

The press release describing your album should be informative and accurate. Never overhype your talents. Even if you think it's true, most execs or reviewers do not want to hear that you're "rock guitar's heir apparent to the Hendrix throne" or "the most innovative jazz trumpeter since Miles Davis." Chances are they have just opened three other packages promising similar sonic thrills. Arrogant and overblown descriptions of your music will only elicit snorts of laughter around the office. Granted, no artist wants to neatly categorize his or her music, but it's necessary that the recipient of your press kit get an idea of your sound. So if it's rock music, call it that; if it's new age, so be it. Music press editors, for example, find such basic information helpful because they need to know which reviewer to give the CD to. Or, for example, a magazine editor might be working on a story about a certain genre; if your music fits the bill, he or she will certainly give it a listen right away, rather than relegating it to the "listen to later" pile.

Most press releases cite musical influences that show through on the album, but if you're not comfortable drawing comparisons to other musicians, explore different ways of getting your point across. Try to write about how your music is supposed to make the listener feel. An energized, driving rock number could be described as "perfect road-trip music." Or a cool jazz track with a melodic lead sax could be called "the first thing you'll want to put on the CD player after a long week at the office." Or a hard-edged techno-metal song could be described as "screaming, pulsing sonic depravity for the truly tortured soul." Well, okay, maybe that last one was a little over the top, but you get the point. The idea is to put yourself in the chair of the person reading about your band. Think about what's going to make them understand your artistic goals and make them want to listen to your music.

One no-no is using so many wildly divergent adjectives that the person reading the description has no idea of what the music could possibly sound like. Be practical. Who's going to want to listen to a CD that's described as "a musical potpourri of Chilean wind instruments and blue grass licks, painted on a backdrop of hip urban grooves"? Even if your music is unusual and hard to categorize, try to give the person reading the press release a reasonable idea of what to expect.

*The idea is to put yourself
in the chair of the person reading
about your band.*

SEEKING COVER

Your cover letter should be short and to the point. Type a concise note introducing yourself, stating what materials are enclosed, contact information, and any other points not made in the press kit itself, such as dates you will be playing in the area. It's a good idea to get a name or a person's title to send your information to. That way you know your music is getting into the right hands, and you can follow up to make sure the package was received.

Be sure your letter is targeted to the right audience. For example, don't send a letter requesting a review to a magazine that doesn't do them or to a publication that doesn't cover your style of music. If you plan to do a big mailing, write a few different stock letters—one for reviewers, one for radio stations, one for labels, and so on—inserting the name of the contact person on the appropriate letter. Do not ask for your materials back because it probably won't happen. If you cannot afford to send out hundreds of press kits, narrow your focus by carefully researching and targeting your destinations.

Each page of your press kit should be on letterhead with your record label or band name, address, phone, fax, and e-mail and Web addresses. This creates a professional appearance and provides a handy reference for those who wish to contact you. If you don't want to invest in letterhead, you can make it on a word processor or at least approximate the effect by putting your contact information at the top or bottom of each page. If your home telephone number is your contact number, be sure your answering machine's outgoing message mentions your band name.

FINISHING TOUCHES

Now that we've discussed the written aspects of your press kit, let's not forget the most important element: the music itself. Always send out the best quality product you can afford. If this is a total DIY effort, plenty of books and periodicals are dedicated to getting the most from your equipment, so do your homework and create a well-produced album. Don't scrimp on the cover art either; it plays a crucial role as the packaging that draws the eye to your music.

CDs are the format of choice these days, as most reviewers and radio stations don't want to deal with cassettes. They also look slicker and more professional than cassettes; furthermore, they sound better and are easier to play and track from. Again, if you're concerned about costs, it's always wiser to distribute a smaller quantity of a better product.

Once you've pulled together the basics for your promo package, you can add a few nice touches. I know that I've lectured about "keeping it simple," but that doesn't mean your kit has to be dull. Artistic touches such as interesting paper and ink colors, elegant fonts, and cool logos go a long way in catching a person's attention. Also, consider getting stickers printed with your band's name or logo on them. You can put these on the outside of the

Even if your music is unusual and hard to categorize, try to give the person reading the press release a reasonable idea of what to expect.

folder that will house your diligently crafted music and prose.

If you're adventurous, you can experiment with interesting packaging, which will almost always pique the recipient's interest enough to get opened first. I've received lovely hand-constructed boxes and mailing envelopes that really stood out in that day's pile. One band sent a CD in packaging that was held together with a large nut and bolt that went through the center of the CD. That was a great example of a simple but attention-getting approach to music packaging.

Bribes also work wonders. I'm not talking about payola but little gimmicks like CD openers, key chains, magnets, matchbooks, and other marketing trinkets. These should all have your band's name or logo on them. Fun items like these tend to stay on the recipients' desks, thus keeping your name in their faces.

But no amount of loot can offset the damage done by a poorly assembled press kit. While writing this chapter I've reflected on what draws me to certain releases. It always comes down to well-written copy and a professional looking CD. In the end, it's the music that counts, but it's necessary that I be intrigued enough to want to listen to it. Your goal in creating the perfect promo package is letting industry pros know that you care enough about your music to try to convince other people to care about it too.

CHAPTER 8

Making Contact

In the music industry, who you know can be more important than what you know, but few musicians start their careers with a direct line to the "star-makers." Fortunately, this limited access often saves new artists the embarrassment of acting unprofessionally in the presence of label executives. The truth is, many talented, creative individuals have no clue about professional interaction with business people. Such ignorance is deadly because poor people skills are every bit as detrimental to career advancement as poor musicianship.

Developing music business contacts is an art form that requires as much creative discipline as songwriting. Getting powermongers to take your calls (and maybe even remember your name) takes time, patience, and thousands of handshakes. So how do you impress these big record-biz big-wigs? Well, as with most endeavors, you start at the bottom and work your way up, which explains why every "overnight" success is usually ten years in the making.

YOUR FIRST FRIENDS

New artists should consider increasing their industry stature when they meet a few of the following criteria: consistent headline or mid-slot status in professional clubs, completion of a professional demo tape or CD, and the interest and support of a performing rights organization (ASCAP, BMI, SESAC, etc.).

Let's start at the beginning. Believe it or not, the people you contact to secure gigs can plant the seeds of your success. You might consider club booking agents to be the bottom fish on the recording-industry food chain, but they are usually your first professional allies in the music business. Bookers get the word out about which bands are hot, and A&R reps (record-label employees who seek out new talent) depend on them for tips on emerging musical trends.

Getting the attention of a booking agent is relatively easy. Generally, all that's needed is a demo, a photo, and a one-page biography. This promo package helps the booker determine whether an act's musical style fits their club format (alternative rock, country, folk, heavy metal, etc.). At this early career juncture, don't bust the bank account on promotional materials, just put together a very basic press kit. However, don't scrimp on professionalism. Developing solid relationships with industry people requires large doses of courtesy, dependability, and a willingness to go the extra mile. In short, don't blow a valuable contact by being a jerk. Most bookers only accept calls during certain hours on certain days, so adhere to this schedule when seeking permission to submit a promo package. Follow up with polite calls (once a week will do) to inquire about your status. Be charming. Be nice. Be persistent. Be patient.

When you get the gig, help the club sell tickets by promoting the show. Send flyers to the fans on your mailing list, bug the local music paper to publicize the show, and tell all

The combination of talent, professionalism, and a high level of visibility will help you make the kind of solid contacts that you need to progress with your career.

your friends. And remember, the show is *never* over. When you load out after the performance, be sure to thank the entire club staff, from door-person to stage manager. Not only is this common courtesy, it's smart. If the booker enjoys working with you, he or she may initiate the first buzz that entices labels to check out your act.

THE TAPE CONTACT

Exploiting a local reputation to obtain record company interest requires enlarging your sphere of contacts beyond the club scene. To accomplish this, you need a more tangible measure of your talents than live performances and rehearsal tapes. A professional demo is your ticket to the next level of the industry.

The very nature of recording a professional demo offers opportunities for important contacts. For one, the studio manager at a recording facility is a valuable asset. Record labels realize that studios are resources for tomorrow's chart-toppers. Many executives keep in touch with engineers and managers whose opinions they respect.

A reputable producer is another valuable contact, and you should not begin a serious demo project without one. A professional demo often is the main arbiter of an act's commercial promise, and it is too important to your success to gamble on self-production (unless you're a registered musical visionary) or semi-pro direction from band buddies or live sound persons. The ears and experience of

a professional who is sensitive to your musical vision are essential to producing a successful demo.

Working producers also have a "down-the-line" advantage: they often have forged their own relationships with label executives and can get your demo directly to the decision-makers. If all goes well, the producer can hand-deliver your tickets to paradise.

BE RELIABLE, BE GOOD

One of the keys to making contacts is to stay active in your local music scene. Play out as much as possible, jam with other musicians, go to clubs to check out other bands, and so on. The more you're out there meeting people and working, the more solid contacts you stand to make.

It's very important that you impress people you meet in working situations; you want them to respect you enough to recommend you for other gigs and possibly to industry execs. After all, when someone gives your name out, they are putting themselves on the line and have to be confident that you'll be able to handle the job. If you screw up, it not only hurts your reputation, but theirs as well. With that in mind, there are two important traits you must possess if you want to make solid connections in the industry.

First and foremost, you must be talented. You don't have to be a virtuoso, but you need to be a solid player and know what's expected for your instrument in whatever genre you're

Treat everyone you meet with respect,
from the lowest door-person to the president
of a record company.

playing. You must also know how to play with other musicians in an ensemble context. If you sound good and make those around you sound better, you're much more likely to engender the respect (and future recommendations) of your bandmates.

The other area where you need to impress your fellow players is with your professionalism. Showing up on time (or better yet, early), staying sober during your gigs, and always bringing the proper gear will help you build a reputation as a solid pro. You'll also help yourself immensely by treating the musicians around you with respect and keeping your ego under control. The combination of talent, professionalism, and a high level of visibility will help you make the kind of solid contacts that you need to progress with your career.

INDUSTRY DECORUM

As we just discussed, a large part of developing industry relationships involves earning respect. When your networking begins to pay off and you meet with a label representative, be polite and engaging. Do some research and find out what other bands he or she works with and what type of acts the label is known for (R&B, alternative, avant-garde, heavy rock, commercial pop, etc.). Use this knowledge as a common thread of conversation. Do not talk about yourself ad nauseam or try to hard-sell your band.

Preliminary contacts with industry professionals should follow accepted rules of courtship. Update your promotional package with your latest demo or release and call the lawyer, manager, or other representative you are pursuing to ask if they are accepting demos and/or new clients. If the answer is yes, type a short cover letter to the person you spoke with (never scrawl a handwritten message on a scrap of paper; you might think it looks charming, but it's not very effective) and send the package. Always follow up with a phone call ten to fourteen days later. Be polite. Be professional. Invite them to your shows. If there is any interest on their part, arrange a business meeting.

When you take this business meeting, be punctual, well-groomed, polite, and professional. Be prepared to explain your vision of creative and financial success. Ask specific questions regarding client rosters and industry contacts. Listen closely to what the representative says and trust your instincts.

It also pays to keep a log of everyone you meet in the industry, from club bookers to engineers to label reps. Just because a lawyer or manager passes on you doesn't mean you shouldn't keep them informed about your progress. They may reconsider their decision or forward your name to another industry contact. Be sure to use the log to chart the successes of the people listed. Everyone appreciates recognition of their work. If you see a contact at a show, compliment them on their latest triumph, and don't miss the opportunity to update them on your career.

The more you're out there meeting people and working, the more solid contacts you stand to make.

CLOSING NOTES

Initial industry interest always means more work: improving your live show, writing better songs, producing yet another demo, and so on.

I can't stress how important it is to treat every aspect of your career professionally. If you act flaky, it will be a struggle getting people to take you seriously. Treat everyone you meet with respect, from the lowest door-person to the president of a record company. You never know, in two years that door-person could be a record company president—and vice versa!

CHAPTER 9

Shopping Your Demo

In recording studios around the world, artists slave over take after take, rewriting, performing, editing, and meticulously crafting their work into demos. Artists trade these precious jewels for the rewards that come with music-industry deals. But before these demos can be exchanged for fame, fortune, and aggressive distribution and promotion, they must first get past the gatekeepers to the Promised Land, those recording-industry executives who listen to music, evaluate talent, and make the deals.

In an effort to demystify the demo-shopping ordeal, I have put together an overview of how the evaluation process works, from the *other* side of the desk. Then, with that groundwork out of the way, we'll discuss how and where to shop your work.

How do they get the music to evaluate? Most industry execs will only accept "solicited submissions" or referrals, which usually means it's coming from a source they know and trust, such as a manager, attorney, or artist they are currently working with. Unsolicited means they have had no prior contact with the act. None of this means that you're completely out in the cold if you don't have a high-powered team behind you, although that never hurts. Publishing and label execs are always on the lookout for new talent, so if you do meet a rep at a showcase or seminar and you hit it off, they may ask you to send along your demo as a follow up. That definitely counts as "solicited."

What do they listen for? What A&R and publishing execs listen for varies greatly depending on the situation. For example, the intent of a songwriter demo is to showcase the lyrics and melody lines of the songs. Most execs don't like a lot of production on these types of demos; they prefer just an acoustic instrument—usually guitar—and the vocal. This approach allows them to evaluate the content and quality of the song's basic elements. On the other hand, artist demos—for those seeking performer deals—should really showcase the artist's talent and style.

Most execs listen by themselves, either in the office or in their cars, but they often solicit second opinions from colleagues and friends. Some labels even have listening committees that are made up of A&R people and other staff members.

TAKING THE HEAT

The reason some musicians cower at the prospect of shopping their work is simple: submitting demo tapes to industry pros is an excruciating experience. It is not an A&R person's job to deliver polite comments about unsuitable material or nurture your commercially unproven talents. If you don't have what it takes to make it in the business, they're not shy about telling you.

Here's a quick reality check. The entertainment business is a profit-driven industry, and record executives are commissioned to find marketable artists and/or songs that will

*Publishing companies are
often-overlooked pathways
to a record deal.*

increase a label's revenues. The music industry is not run by artists for the sole purpose of enriching society; it is directed by corporate business interests who crave profit margins wider than the Grand Canyon.

Locked in mortal combat with the balance sheet, an A&R executive's job security is often measured in minutes. Signing one artist that doesn't meet sales projections can mean the "former" executive ends up working at K-Mart before the next *Billboard* hits the newsstands. This situation explains why many A&R people should be excused for not empathizing with your artistic pain and suffering. Give them hits and maybe they'll give you a shoulder to cry on.

Furthermore, few musicians understand that pursuing a commercial music career opens the deepest chambers of your soul to the often witless criticism of The Public. The bottom line is, if you can't take a punch or you don't care about monetary success (no shame in that), you're excused from reading the rest of this chapter.

DOING THE DEED

Okay, you've survived the horror stories. Now let's get to work. There is a definite procedure for submitting demos to industry professionals, and you're better off playing by the rules in this particular situation. People rarely get points for messing with professional etiquette. Here are some basic pointers on getting your demo into the right hands.

Ask permission. Never send a demo without first getting approval. Even if a music publisher claims to accept unsolicited material, be courteous and forward a query letter before you send off your package. Query letters should be typewritten and include the contact person's full name. ("To whom it may concern" is not an appropriate greeting.) Do not include your creative history in the text of the letter. Simply state that you are seeking permission to submit a demo package consisting of, for example, three songs. Make sure to include a self-addressed and stamped reply postcard.

Send a clear message. If you receive permission to submit your work, compile a well-documented package. First, type a brief cover letter thanking the contact person for his or her interest. Be concise. If a biography is requested, make it short (one or two paragraphs is ideal) and include a black and white, 8 x 10 glossy photo. Be sure that your name, address, and telephone number are marked on the tape or CD cover and on the cassette or CD itself. (See chapter 7, "Seductive Promotion.")

Follow up. Two weeks after you mail the package, call the contact person to confirm receipt of your materials. Do not badger them or seek a personal critique over the telephone. Their jobs entail a lot more work than just listening to demos, and you'll only get on their bad side if you bother them. If they haven't received your package, politely say that you'll check again in another week.

It is not an A&R person's job to deliver polite comments about unsuitable material or nurture your commercially unproven talents.

Always be sure that your package makes it into the right hands.

And again, if you are fortunate enough to get your demo into an exec's hands, don't call every couple of days looking for feedback. Once you've confirmed that the package was received, you can check back in three or four weeks. That's the standard in the business, and most industry pros won't be put off by that kind of follow up. In fact they expect it.

But, honestly, if they like what they hear, *they'll* call you. These professionals' careers depend on the discovery and exploitation of new talent. If they think you have something special to offer, they'll be in touch. Execs rarely call back with rejects. They have so many hundreds of demos to deal with that they don't have the time to do that. Again, this is why it's important to get your music to them through known channels. If you used a manager or lawyer to deliver the demo and the execs have an established relationship with that person, they'll be able to tell them frankly why they're not interested. It's just part of the business. Managers, agents, and attorneys are used to dealing with this stuff, so let them do their jobs.

Be gracious. If an industry pro rejects your demo, type them a short letter thanking them for their time and consideration. Professionals appreciate such common courtesy—even if they don't reply—and may remember your name fondly when you ask to submit your next demo. (You weren't thinking of giving up after one try, were you?)

If they like what they hear. What happens if they like your work depends on who it is that likes your demo. If you're shopping an artist deal to a label, you might get signed to a record contract. If you're a singer/songwriter, a publisher might want to sign you to a publishing deal and pitch your songs to acts looking for tunes. Or if you've submitted an artist demo to a publisher, you might get a publishing deal and the publisher might refer you to a colleague at a record label. Again, it depends on what you're looking for, how professional you are, and how much you have to offer. Your chances are always better if you have management, an attorney, and other elements of a professional team behind you.

PATHS OF GLORY

Now that you know the procedure, you need to know where to send your music. Some of these ideas are obvious, but I've included a few practical insights for each option. Do not hope for a home run on your first time out. Think of it as building a dialog with the industry. If an exec thinks you have talent, they'll *ask* you to stay in touch.

Record labels. A direct submission to a record company puts the chances of scoring a deal into the same statistical stratosphere as breaking the bank at Monte Carlo. But people *do* get signed, so why not you? However, be smart. Don't "shotgun submit" to every label in the world. Such lunacy only wastes time and money. Do some market research and

Furthermore, few musicians understand that pursuing a commercial music career opens the deepest chambers of your soul to the often witless criticism of The Public.

determine which labels routinely exploit your style of music. Once you've narrowed the market focus, religiously follow all rules of demo submission, especially getting permission. Remember that in seeking notice from overworked A&R departments, one misstep equals doom.

Music publishers. Publishing companies are often-overlooked pathways to a record deal. Many publishers sign up promising artists and producers—as long as they can write their own material—and help them seek record contracts. The payback is obvious: A full album of artist-penned tunes can generate sizable revenue because the publisher is entitled to publishing royalties based on sales and airplay. To distinguish yourself from the legions of nonperforming songwriters seeking staff writing or single-song deals, be sure to include the appropriate "slashes" in your submission letter (e.g., producer/songwriter, artist/songwriter, artist/producer/songwriter, and so on).

Management firms. Good managers constantly look toward the future. A firm may represent today's hottest acts, but today's superstars often turn into tomorrow's has-beens. Ambitious artists can win a manager's support by nurturing a casual relationship based on increasingly commercial demos.

Entertainment lawyers. Some music attorneys aspire to be artist managers, record company executives, and even producers. Of course, pulling off such a career change requires a marketable "flagship" artist. Get

the picture? But even if a music lawyer doesn't become directly involved in your career, he or she can refer you to valuable industry contacts. It pays to keep reputable attorneys updated on your career, but beware of less-dignified lawyers who charge fees to listen to demos. If they're seriously looking for acts to shop or develop, they should listen to your demo for free.

Performance rights societies. ASCAP, BMI, and SESAC offer many services to aspiring songwriters and recording artists, including new-music concerts that showcase unsigned artists to the industry. In addition, each society has executives who routinely monitor up-and-coming artists. Make sure these people have your latest demo. A&R executives often seek counsel from these societies, so it pays to be the next name on their lips when the labels call.

Songwriter associations. Songwriter associations can be life buoys for frustrated composers. If you're having difficulty getting industry pros to listen to your material, most songwriter associations sponsor events—often called "demo derbies" or "cassette roulette"—where members can play their demos face-to-face with A&R executives or publishers. In addition, many associations also sponsor open-mic performances and songwriter conferences. Nonmembers can usually check out events for a nominal fee.

Go online. Check out your online options for shopping your demo. There are music-promotion sites and online record

Your chances are always better if you have management, an attorney, and other elements of a professional team behind you.

labels that offer access to music executives. Bear in mind, though, that having your own or being a part of someone else's site does not guarantee that anyone of import will see you or hear your music. If you're truly out for a record deal, you're better off using one of the tried and true methods mentioned above and supplementing it with an online presence. And even then, you're probably wise to deal with an established online entity, such as IUMA (Internet Underground Music Archive) or Billboard's TalentNet. There is usually a fee for these types of services.

Talk to your peers to find out what sites are hot and whether they know of anyone who has actually been "discovered" on one of these sites. The benefit of an online presence is that anyone can check out clips of your music at anytime and they can contact you via e-mail if they like what they hear.

FINAL FADE

Most musicians can take solace in the fact that every successful artist was trashed by someone. However, it can take months, or even years, between submitting your first demo and the signing of your first contract. You should also take into account that when record industry execs like something enough to take a risk on it, they are putting their professional reputations on the line. They have to be convinced that you're worth the risk.

When you approach the process of shopping your demo, consider these four points.

First, know what kind of presentation you are trying to make. Are you an artist? A songwriter? A producer? Prepare your presentation accordingly. Second, network, network, network your way to someone who knows the inside player you are trying to get to. Attorneys, managers, and people who are working within the organization you are interested in are the best avenues. Third, have respect for the time constraints your listener is under. And finally, do not lose faith for a minute or stop working at making your talents shine. Perseverance is critical: Keep writing, keep improving, keep submitting your work. If you give up, you're finished.

CHAPTER 10

Exposing Yourself

If you want any measure of success in the music business—be it money, fame, or simply the chance to make a decent living playing music—people have to know about you. Sure, that's a pretty simple and obvious statement, but getting your name and your music known among your peers, the media, and local club-goers and record buyers is a lot of work. The basic steps in gaining exposure for your band are creating a press kit, letting the media and the public know what you're up to, and working, working, working. In fact, the more you gig and stay involved in your local music community, the more familiar fans and media will be with your name and your music.

FEEDING THE MEDIA

Your first step is to assemble a press kit. In simple terms, a press kit is a promotional tool that tells the media what you want them to say about you. Believe it or not, the information that ends up in magazines and newspapers is often lifted verbatim from press kits. (See chapter 7, "Seductive Promotion.)

Each item in the press kit should accurately represent your style and image. Do not misrepresent yourself because it will undoubtedly come back to haunt you. In the same vein, try to keep superlatives out of your press materials. Media people get hundreds of press releases a week touting the "best," the "greatest," and the "most talked about." You won't fool anyone with self-praise. Bravado is boring, and unproven bravado is pathethic.

A common mistake many musicians make when they first start seeking publicity is not understanding the workings of the press. Do your homework before engaging in a promotional campaign. This means researching which magazines and trade papers might be interested in what you're doing. It's important to find out who to call. A typical magazine or newspaper has many different editors with different functions. For example, a calendar editor is only interested in *who, what, when,* and *where*. However, a feature editor seeks longer, general interest stories and usually requires a press kit and a news "hook" to determine if your band is worthy of coverage.

Also, be sure to find out publication deadlines and work within them. (Many magazines have lead times of two to three months, so notifying them a week before an event is pointless.) Don't forget that media professionals are extremely busy, so be respectful of their time. Good publicists limit follow-up calls to concise discussions that take no more than a couple of minutes from "Hello" to hang-up. Don't limit your efforts to print coverage: try to land radio and TV appearances on local talk shows and small independent or public-access channels.

The basic press kit items mentioned above should be sufficient for mailings to the media, but if you want to send your kit to prospective clients, such as corporate party planners and so on, you should also include a business card and videotape. A video can be a

Even if you're a great player, people will not be willing to hire you if you have a bad attitude.

strong sales tool because it allows prospective clients to actually see you perform. Also consider creating a Web page. With the software available, you can do a simple Web page yourself that you can update regularly with new gigs or other band information. Potential clients can visit your site any time to see what you have to offer. Put your Web and e-mail addresses on your business cards, which you should *always* have with you.

Now, with all your tools in place, how do you get people to notice you?

EXPOSURE THROUGH PLAYING

Just as it takes money to make money, you have to play gigs to get gigs. Not only does playing clubs, parties, benefits, and other events help pay the bills, it goes a long way in creating a great word of mouth buzz for your band. It's also important to remember that some gigs might not seem like great opportunities in themselves, but they can lead to other, better paying and higher profile gigs down the line. Let's look at the ways you can build up a good reputation and get your act out in the marketplace and in the media. And, honestly, no matter how much you want to play music for the sake of art, you should plan to devote at least half of your time to marketing.

Word of mouth. Put yourself in the shoes of a booking agent or a professional event planner for a moment. When these pros book a performer, they are putting their own repu-

tations on the line; they have to trust the performers they call on to be professional and make the client happy. They could search for performers by checking out ads in the local music press or by going through the numerous promotional materials they've amassed, but they'd rather call on a known quantity, someone they have worked with before or have seen perform. If they do ever call outside the group of performers they're familiar with, it's because the band has something really special to offer. Word of mouth is the most potent form of advertising. Think of it like this: if you have to go to the dentist, would you rather call someone out of the phone book or someone a friend went to and liked?

Versatility. The first thing to do is to focus on what you have to offer. Think about why someone should hire you over another band and what it is that makes you attractive to an audience. Do you appeal to specific niches? Maybe you can play Irish tunes for step dancers, polka tunes for a folk dancer's party, or klezmer tunes for a bar mitzvah. Or perhaps you have Victorian costumes for a Christmas caroling gig or Renaissance costumes for a fair. The more versatile you are, the more gigs you can get. If you have a rock 'n' roll or jazz band, consider forming an acoustic or semiacoustic offshoot that can be booked for smaller venues and quieter situations, such as weddings. (If your act is really versatile in this way, you can play quiet, acoustic pieces for the ceremony and pop music for dancing at the reception.)

No matter how much you want to play music for the sake of art, you should plan to devote at least half of your time to marketing.

Benefits. As a general rule, play benefits. Although they rarely pay much (if anything), they are great publicity and help you network with other bands. They also give you an opportunity to play large venues with nice stages and good sound systems.

If no one calls you for a benefit, find out when one is happening and call the organizer. Offer to help with other aspects of the event if you can; a good attitude and a helping hand can get you just as far as hours of practicing. And if there isn't a benefit happening, create one! Think of some charities or other organizations that you're interested in helping, and organize a benefit for them. Another idea is to coproduce concerts with local college radio stations. Cross-promotional efforts are a great way to approach getting more exposure for your band. Be forewarned about organizing such benefits and concerts, though. These can be wonderful events, but they are a huge amount of work to produce and publicize.

Be sure to promote your participation in any such event well before the show date; these happenings are great fodder for print, radio, and television coverage. Also, include any reviews of the show or articles about the benefit in your press clippings.

Group and corporate parties. Most cities have organizations such as business associations, church leagues, fraternal lodges, and cultural groups, and every organization has parties at one time or another. Once you have played even one successful gig for an organization, you will probably be asked back for more and maybe for their friends, too. They might ask you to do a small gig for a good cause for free, such as playing a birthday party for a revered older citizen. Consider doing a few of these; they can be very rewarding in future possibilities. And learn a few special tunes if they want you to. After all, having a few waltzes in the repertoire never hurts.

Don't forget corporate parties. Most businesses have occasional or seasonal parties. These types of events often pay extremely well. In this case, knowing someone who works for the company can get your foot in the door. Make sure all your friends are familiar with your music and realize that you're available for these types of events.

Most metropolitan areas have a convention and visitors bureau. This kind of organization often suggests entertainers, caterers, and other support personnel for major events. Sometimes they have mixers at which performers and caterers show off their wares to a large number of invited potential clients. Getting a spot to play at one of these mixers can lead to some great connections.

Something a little different. Consider aligning yourself with people in ancillary fields, such as independent filmmakers, performance artists, theater groups, or multimedia and game developers. Not only does your work get exposure to people who might not have discovered it otherwise, you get to work in an exciting new arena with endless promotional possibilities.

*Once you have played even one successful gig
for an organization, you will probably be asked back
for more and maybe for their friends, too.*

A mixed-media collaboration is another way of distinguishing your act from others; especially if you perform in a unique venue such as a museum or photo gallery. A sense of "something different" *is* newsworthy. Face it, local club gigs are great for honing your act and developing chops, but they're not exactly hot news.

Your reputation. Your reputation can be the most important thing you possess. In fact, the image developed by a business is so important that it is recognized as a legitimate asset by the United States legal system. It is also a very important aspect of what we're talking about here. Whatever you do, don't get a reputation as being unreliable or a problem child; that kind of bad rep gets around quickly. Even if you're a great player, people will not be willing to hire you if you have a bad attitude. It is wise to be on your best behavior, whether you're on stage or off.

When you're working, always turn on the charm and remain calm, even if the client is frantic or angry, and don't let them know that you have any qualms about your own performance. If they like you, just thank them graciously; and if they don't realize you played an F sharp instead of an F natural, don't tell them. Also, know the protocol: if the event's booking agent wants you to give out exclusively his or her business card and not quote rates, then make sure you follow those instructions.

Emergencies happen and sometimes you have to scramble to find players to sit in, but if you do have to cancel, make sure you have alternate suggestions for someone to cover for you. Helping out in that way will be remembered. Sometimes, if a gig isn't quite up your alley, you can help find a more appropriate performer for an agent. This helpfulness, too, increases your reputation in a positive way.

FUTURE PLANS

Sit down and do some long-range planning. Think many months ahead when planning any promotions. Your main goal is to make your connections in the music community and the media work for you. All it takes is energy, tenacity, and a little help from your friends. And don't get discouraged if one avenue proves a dead end. There are many ways to get attention, and different things work for different people.

CHAPTER 11

Timing Your Release

The artistic process is subtle and introspective and not necessarily subject to the constraints of time. When it comes to your music, you can spend all the time you desire wringing the last drops of genius from your soul to create a musical masterpiece. But getting this brilliant piece of work into the hands of the public is very much a matter of timing. You have to obtain distribution, get into retail outlets, and promote your CD.

Whether you are releasing a record yourself, on a small independent label, or on a major, your success is dependent on how you work the system and time the various elements of your release. In fact, you should create a marketing plan for your release *before* you even start recording. Because majors and major independents take care of most of the work of releasing a new record for you, we'll focus here on the artist who is going it alone or working with a small label. Also, this is an overview of the process of releasing an album; more in-depth information on the specifics is given in subsequent chapters.

The steps outlined here are not necessarily chronological; every element in a CD release is dependent on the timing of the other elements. In general, you want to start by planning the CD's street date, then work backwards from there to plan distribution and promotion. When your CD hits the street, several different forces should be converging at the same time, all preplanned and appropriately timed.

BEWARE, BE AWARE

The past few years have been turbulent for the entire music industry. Consumers are buying more music, but record stores and labels are going out of business at an alarming rate. One reason for this massive shakeup is the glut of CDs on the market. That's the down side of being able to produce CD-quality recordings in our homes: just about everybody who can release a CD does so, filling distributor warehouses and retail shelves with too much product. Retailers are stuck with huge inventories of CDs that don't sell and are forced to return them to distributors, who then return them to the labels (many of whom then lose their distribution and file for bankruptcy).

So take heed: in this time of upheaval, the best way to approach your career is to get back to basics, create a grass roots regional infrastructure, and build up slowly from there. As the market stabilizes, the artists and labels that have vision and patience will survive. The bottom line is to have great music and to produce the very best CD that you possibly can. With sufficient talent and a solid, well-informed business plan, you have a much better chance of success.

MANUFACTURING

Part of your time line should include the process of manufacturing your CD, including the printing of your cover art. You should finish

*In-store appearances
are a great way to work
your release.*

the artwork for your project early enough to include it in mailings to your distributor and to use in teaser postcards and so on.

It takes an average of six to eight weeks to design and manufacture a new title and about two weeks to re-run an existing title. Remember to include shipping time, too. Shipping varies depending on the service, but it usually takes from five to ten days. Give yourself leeway just to be on the safe side.

DISTRIBUTION

You must have distribution in place before you release your CD. Without it, you have a closet full of CDs that you can sell only at gigs or online. Suffice it to say that without distribution there is little reason to engage in a full-scale CD promotional campaign. You will simply be spending a lot of money for minimal product branding. Getting airplay or advertising doesn't do any good if your record isn't readily available to the buyer. It's very difficult to get distribution these days if you are an unsigned and unestablished act, but it's not impossible. I strongly recommend that you budget the funds to hire a full-service music promotion firm to get you in the back door and nail down a distribution deal.

Submit your new title to your distributor no later than three months prior to the street date; send a copy of the final mix on cassette or CD-R along with the artwork as soon as you have both. This timing is imperative because distributors have catalog and other deadlines

that they have to meet. You definitely want to be included in the monthly or bi-monthly publications they put out. Also, send copies of the CD to the distributor's sales reps as soon as possible, for they are the ones who will be selling it to the retailers. Stay in touch with them, develop strong relationships, and keep abreast of how your CD is doing.

PROMOTION

The old-fashioned method of putting together a strong live act, honing it until it sparkles, and then gigging as often as possible is still the best method of promoting yourself. Whether you're a blues band, a trance/techno ensemble, or a solo act, getting on the stage and performing killer shows is the surest way to generate a buzz about your music. There's simply no better way to improve your odds of achieving success.

Playing live should be an on-going effort, but I highly recommend that you save the big tour for *after* your record release, hitting the appropriate cities and towns at the same time that your other promos are peaking in those areas. Work out the timing so that any co-op advertising between your label and distributor—and any other print or radio advertising—is running in the local media when you get into town to perform.

As a rule, print advertising doesn't work unless you are a major artist and/or have the budget to sustain an ongoing ad campaign in a highly visible publication over a long period

Be persistent but nice;
learn to become a
"pleasant nuisance."

of time. However, selective, niche-market advertising—such as running an ad in a bass magazine if you are releasing a solo bass record or a new age publication if you are a new age artist—can be beneficial. But if you are going to run print ads, consult closely with the ad departments. Most major magazines will need your ad copy at least three months before your street date.

RETAIL

Timely retail promotion is another important aspect of releasing a CD. A month to two weeks prior to the street date, send promo copies of your release to your key retail accounts for in-store play. This is an excellent way to promote your music: customers browsing the store will hear your CD and, hopefully, will want to buy it. Make sure you send it to the appropriate buyer for your style of music because they will be the ones who will play it. If the new age buyer ends up with a grunge CD, it probably won't get played. In-store play also gives store managers a chance to hear your music.

A good retail promotion is posters or postcards advertising the CD. The store manager can put posters on the walls or place smaller cards near the registers for people to pick up. You should also send copies of your one-pagers with blank boxes at the bottom that the retailers can fill in with their own store information. A one-pager (also called a one-sheet) is an 8.5 x 11–inch sheet of paper

that provides a synopsis of your release. One-pagers can be done very simply or in elaborate color graphics. As a rule, they should contain the name of the act, the title of the release, the street date, the bar code, some sort of graphic representation of the CD, the name of the record label, catalog number, and a written summary (without too much hype) of the music. These one-pagers are what the distributor and retailers use to order product. They also make nice flyers. Send them in bulk to the retailers 30 days before your street date to help them support your release and facilitate faster reorders.

In-store appearances are a great way to work your release. Being physically present in a Borders Books or Tower Records store playing your songs while the CD is sitting there on the shelves produces immediate results: people hear you, they like you, and they buy your CD. Promote in-store performances with posters and flyers at least three weeks before the show. Another great PR tool is online concerts. Just make sure that all of these elements fall into the time period around the street date of your release.

RADIO

Radio play is key to the success of your CD. This is where playing live figures heavily. If your band is going to be playing in an area and has generated interest there, then radio will be much more receptive to you. Be aware that radio does not always back-announce

Getting on the stage and performing killer shows is the surest way to generate a buzz about your music.

information on the song just played (e.g., what label the record is on and where it's available), so it's up to you to have advertising and publicity lined up to support the airplay.

New artists should release a record after the first of the year, preferably in February or March. Avoid May and January because college radio stations turn over their staffs during those months. Send CDs—and only CDs—no more than 30 days prior to the street date. Do not send shrink-wrapped CDs; you want your disc to be as accessible as possible. Also, punch holes in the cover and write the station call letters on it bold ink. Otherwise, your release may end up at the used CD store. Send the CDs to the music director, and include the track-sheet description. Also, find out the music director's hours for calls. Music directors are usually only available a couple of days a week, a couple of hours each day.

Make plenty of follow-up calls. Simply sending your CD to the radio station and calling once or twice won't work. Be persistent but nice; learn to become a "pleasant nuisance." Again, this is a job for professional radio promoters. These pros make their living by knowing the DJs at different stations and when to call. Bear in mind, though, that radio is ancillary. Just getting radio play alone doesn't mean much; if the records aren't in the stores at the time of the airplay, your return is going to be minimal.

PUBLICITY

Be prepared to send out a lot of promotional copies of the CD to reviewers and other music-media people. The more people that hear your music, the better. If you are looking at a release date in late winter or early spring, you should start generating publicity for your release in the late summer or early fall of the previous year. Everyone in the industry is swamped from September up through December, so give yourself time to get your CD out there and circulating. Hopefully, you'll also get reviews that will run about the time of the street date. Remember that multiple impressions sell CDs, so call as much attention to yourself as early on as you can.

As a rule, you should start your publicity push four months ahead of the street date, although it is beneficial to send out some sort of teaser in the form of postcards or press releases six months ahead of time. All of the major consumer publications require three to six months of lead time for editorial deadlines. Local publications usually need less lead time; contact the paper's editorial office to find out when you need to submit for reviews. Your reviews should coincide with your release date as much as possible.

Be sure to submit press releases to print-media music calendars six weeks to one month prior to any gig you have booked. Most newspapers will not respond to you personally; you merely send a press release to the editor of the calendar section and cross your

Don't make the mistake of waiting until your CDs are finished before making your business plan.

fingers that you are included. If you are a well-known act that has done a lot of pavement pounding already, the editor will welcome any gig information. Furthermore, if you have done a good job of creating a buzz, you can interest journalists in writing feature articles on your band. And regarding calendars, college radio stations have on-air music calendars. So, be sure they are aware of any dates you have coming up.

Also, work with local radio and try to get interviews to correspond with your release. You can do live, on-air performances at some stations in conjunction with your interview. This is great publicity and should be a part of any artist's regional and national efforts. Television—cable, public, and network, if possible—should also be a part of this effort. Local cable-access stations are a good way to get your act on TV in your area.

A TALE OF WOE

A friend told me about a certain release that is a good example of how *not* to work a record. This particular CD was a Christmas album, and a very good one at that. The publicity campaign needed to get underway by June or July in order to have the retailers stocked and the press published during the all-important holiday season.

Unfortunately, this act didn't have a comprehensive written agenda for their record. They didn't get into the studio to record until the beginning of August, they finished record-

ing in September, and the CD wasn't mastered and pressed until mid October. Commercial radio goes soft in October, so if you aren't getting airplay well before then, you are wasting your time and money. The press mailing didn't go out until November 5th—way too late to have any impact.

Apparently, this could have been a popular release because the people who did hear it called the independent label and wanted to know where it was available. It's obviously a good sign when people call to request your CD; what little exposure this CD received still created a demand for it. Nonetheless, the release fell flat and didn't sell many copies.

Had this project been timed properly, with all the elements in place well before Christmas, the record could have sold well. Short of that, the group simply should have been patient and waited until the next year to release the album. Remember, you control the way the public sees your art; no one else has to know that you recorded it the year before.

ALL LINED UP

This is your music. You've worked hard all your life to improve as an artist, playing gig after gig in noisy, smoky clubs in order to hone your skills and get a chance at success. Why, then, do so many musicians focus only on the creative process and fail to think about the bigger picture? Sadly, it appears that many are simply ignorant of the *business* side of

*Work with local radio and try
to get interviews to correspond
with your release.*

music. Don't make the mistake of waiting until your CDs are finished before making your business plan.

The key is patience. Just because a CD is done doesn't mean it is ready to be released. Get opinions from people in the industry first, and try to gain some objective insight as to how your project will do before you spend thousands on promotion. Work on creating a comprehensive and systematic marketing plan. The success of your CD is too important for you to wing it. Even if you use a professional service, the better informed you are, the easier it will be to work with them toward your goal.

Getting Airplay

Like other pathways in a band's career, the road to radio airplay isn't easy. Getting airplay is hard enough for acts with record deals, but it's toughest on bands that don't have a label behind them—but that's not to say it's impossible. Here's a look at what's involved in getting radio stations to play your music, whether you want to do it yourself or use the services of a record promoter.

CALLING ALL STATIONS

Radio stations fall into three general categories: college, commercial, and public. Commercial-free college radio is fertile ground for mainly underground music or as yet unknown bands. These stations occupy a space on the dial where bands can generate a loyal following well before enjoying any commercial success; in fact, airplay on college radio has seriously affected the trajectory of many careers. Every musical style is played on college stations, with an emphasis on new material, which provides more opportunity for new artists than commercial radio does.

Most public stations are not commercially oriented and are therefore not governed solely by ratings. The likelihood of receiving airplay on public radio is better for unknown bands than on commercial radio, but the number of musical programs and outlets for artists is broader on college stations than on public stations.

Commercial stations are concerned primarily with ratings and the advertising revenues those ratings generate. The musical formats are usually homogeneous and strict because DJs must play hits (whether new or old) to keep listeners hooked for extended periods of time. In pop and rock, it's not uncommon for bands to graduate to commercial radio after they've caused some waves in the realm of college radio.

Commercial stations are divided into different stylistic formats, for example, Contemporary Hit Radio (CHR), Album Oriented Rock (AOR), Rap, Country, Adult Contemporary, and so on. Each week, trade publications track stations in every category and compile information for the powerful and influential charts that list records receiving the most national airplay. These charts are vital to a record's success because radio stations are blatant copy cats. When a station sees that a record is "hot" on similarly formatted stations, it often adds the record to their playlist. Then, as more stations add the record, its chart position increases, and the hopeful journey to the top of the charts begins.

THE MEDIUM

Make sure your mastering job is top-notch. You will want the best quality you can afford because a release that sounds amateurish probably will not get played. Format selection is also critical to your chances of getting played on radio. Radio stations don't deal with

Bounce-back cards are a good, inexpensive way to track whether your package was received.

cassette tapes anymore, so plan on pressing CDs. The type of CD you plan to send to radio stations is a function of your band's budget. If you can afford it, consider pressing a CD single—a common radio-promotion format—in addition to pressing a full-length CD for press and retail.

You don't have to break the bank for artwork on the radio versions, however. It's common practice to send radio stations a CD single in a clear jewel box with information only on the disc. So save the fancy insert and cover artwork for the retail version of your release.

RESEARCH

Your first step in pursuing radio airplay should actually occur long before your CD is finished. Register all of your songs with your performing rights society, that way the organization can track your songs and collect the performance royalties should you get airplay.

Once it comes time to send out your release, don't send it indiscriminately to every station you can think of. You should first determine which ones are most receptive to your style of music. Most unknown artists can only afford to send their releases to a small, well-targeted list of stations.

The promotional options facing an artist with an independent or a self-released record are limited. Frankly speaking, most CHR stations only play major-label releases, so it's a waste of time and money to send your release

to them. It is better to get your record happening in a more receptive arena first. College, public, alternative, and other more specialized stations (rap, new age, etc.) usually accept records from smaller independent labels. Commercial stations often keep their eye on these smaller stations to see who's generating any heat.

Radio trade journals come in handy when trying to determine which stations to send your release to. Get a copy of the trades such as *CMJ, The Gavin Report,* or *Billboard.* These publications are read by people who are serious about radio, i.e., program directors, music directors, DJs, radio consultants, and label reps who need to see which releases are receiving airplay. Radio stations report their playlists to the trades, and the playlists are subsequently compiled into national and regional charts. A station's playlist shows the rotation of a band's airplay, usually broken down into heavy, medium, and add. (Add refers to releases that have been recently added to the playlist and are not yet in heavy or medium rotation.) The charts in the trades are broken down by style of music, such as top 100, rap, country, jazz, and alternative.

Keep in mind that some trades are more genre-specific than others. Depending on their format, specific stations report to specific trades, meaning that not all college or commercial stations will be found in any given trade. The trades also review new releases and sell radio-specific advertising to labels and bands. Depending on your budget,

49
Chapter Twelve

Your first step in pursuing radio airplay should actually occur long before your CD is finished.

and whether you are interested in national exposure on radio, you might want to take out an ad in one or more of the trades. A trade advertisement familiarizes program directors (PDs), music directors (MDs), and DJs with your band's name, which helps set you apart from the hundreds of other bands sending out releases.

If you end up with more stations on your list than originally expected, narrow down the list using some basic demographics. You might want to focus on stations in your area for a local angle on airplay, or you can opt to give preference to stations serving large metropolitan areas. Some trades include the name of the PD or MD and phone number for each station. Because college radio welcomes new artists, it's okay to call them and ask a few questions. (Can I get a copy of your programming guide? Are you likely to play our kind of music? How many watts is your transmitter? What is your address, and to whom should I direct my release?)

THE MAILING

It sounds obvious, but above and beyond all other facts about a band, it's the music that gets them played. A college radio MD will have no difficulty in deciding between a mediocre band that's opened for Pink Floyd and sends out a 10-page press kit and a band with just a one page bio but has a sound that just blows him or her away. That's the beauty of college radio: the DJs have a lot of latitude when it comes to playing what they like, no matter where it comes from. They aren't constricted by set playlists like the commercial stations are.

Because college radio is staffed by students, many of them are gone during summer and winter breaks, and they turn over their staff at the very end of each term. Therefore, it's best to send your music either in late winter/early spring (between winter and spring breaks, e.g., February/March) or well into fall (after the beginning of the school year and before winter break, e.g., September). Along with the record, include in your mailer a letter addressed to the MD with some information about your band. Do not overhype your music or list every band you've ever opened for because the MD probably doesn't care. Suggest a song or two that you think is the most radio friendly. If there are one or two key (and preferably short) pieces of press about your band, include those.

Bounce-back cards are a good, inexpensive way to track whether your package was received. These postcards are stamped and addressed back to you; they ask for the station's name, address, phone number, and the name of the person who listened to the record (or at least opened the package). Ask if the station liked the record enough to add it to their current rotation. Also, have the station list which trades they report to because this is where you might see your song charting.

Even if your music is perfectly suited for a particular station, you still need to get the

Savvy artist managers often negotiate with the labels to hire indies for their clients.

MD or DJ to see your mailing, pick it up, open it, and play it. Once your package arrives at the station, it is added to a pile of packages waiting to be opened. Use your creativity to draw the MD's attention to your record. Homespun and handmade packaging can be an effective eye catcher.

After a few weeks, you'll receive some bounce-back cards. These are the stations that cared enough to respond. Try to make relationships with the MDs or DJs that gave the most favorable feedback. If your band can tour through the towns or cities where you're most appreciated, then call those stations and ask which local clubs they recommend for a show. If they really like your music, you might even be able to negotiate a radio interview or an in-station gig.

RECORD PROMOTERS

If you don't have the time or stomach for the full-on DIY approach to promoting your CD to radio stations, you have the option of hiring a record promoter. A mysterious aura has always surrounded record promoters. If you believe the muckrakers, independent promoters are nothing more than criminals who trade money and drugs for radio airplay. Granted, the music business *does* have its share of borderline characters—at every level—but the majority of record promoters are far from purveyors of payola.

Basically, record promoters are hard-working people immersed in the responsibil-

ity of getting an artist's work out to the public. *How* they work varies from promoter to promoter, but *what* they do is simple: they get records played on the radio.

PROMOTING SUCCESS

Shaking some action on the charts is not an easy gig. Because of the overwhelming number of releases stations receive, merely sending a record to a radio station won't get it played, even if you're Geffen or Columbia. Station PDs and MDs receive at least 50 new records a week. The competition for airtime is brutal. Major labels attack the competition with in-house promotion departments whose sole responsibility is to *personally* deliver records to the radio stations. Promotion staffs also place initial introductory calls to the station describing the current release, make follow-up calls informing the station of the release's current success on other stations, wine and dine PDs and MDs, and develop promotional giveaways and contest trips that enhance the record's appeal to radio personnel and consumers.

However, in-house promotional staffs are often overwhelmed by the sheer number of their label's releases. To effectively work the overflow, labels hire independent record promoters, or *indies*. Indie promoters are specialists who have nurtured close personal and professional relationships with the PDs and MDs of important radio stations. Because the key to good promotion is personal contacts,

*Fate and luck play a huge role
in getting your music heard on the radio,
but hard work is the biggest factor.*

these people are incredibly valuable. They act as a conduit between a label and a station and can get through to a PD or MD when others can't. For example, if 50 promotion reps are calling a station, the PD is most likely to return the calls of people he or she knows, likes, and trusts.

The price for an indie's contacts and persuasive talents varies according to his or her industry standing, success record, the format being promoted, and the type of project. The costs can range from a few hundred dollars to more than one thousand dollars per week for a specified number of weeks, or a flat fee ranging from a few thousand to more than twenty thousand dollars for the "life of the project" (generally considered to be ten weeks).

Savvy artist managers often negotiate with the labels to hire indies for their clients. This is smart business because it ensures that the artist won't get lost in the shuffle of releases promoted by the label. The fee for independent promotion is paid by the artist's promotional budget—which may or may not be recoupable by the label—and the label writes the checks.

PROMOTING SMALL LABELS

Smaller, independent labels perceive chart action differently than the majors. The life of an independent record is not greatly influenced by chart numbers, as the company may only have a regional emphasis or a niche mar-

ket. However, when a small label does chart a record, it greatly increases the label's industry status, credibility, and visibility. Self-released records that chart usually make a big splash at major-label A&R departments.

Exploiting this specific market are a growing number of small indie promoters who work small-label and self-released records. Their radio lists are compiled from some of the specialized trade publications mentioned earlier. Fees paid to the small indie promoter are more in line with independent label budgets, averaging a couple hundred dollars per week, with a four-week minimum. The smaller indies usually commit to calling each station once every two weeks and provide other services such as promotional mailings that are billed separately

Obviously, no large record label is underwriting the promotional costs for self-released or independent projects (unless the label has cut a distribution deal with a major). This means *you* are paying the bills, so be sure to target your radio audience and hire an indie who specializes in your field. And because of the frequent college radio staff turnover, it's nearly impossible to form close bonds with PDs and MDs at those stations, so the value of a smaller indie promoter lies in his or her knowledge of the station's overall programming. A college station's format usually does not change, even if the staff does.

A good, reputable indie promoter should give you a client history that details past successes and a list of stations they service. If you

Record promoters are hard-working people immersed in getting an artist's work out to the public. They get records played on the radio.

hire them, make sure you receive a detailed break down every week of your record's activity on each station. This report should include whether the station listened to the record or not, any comments from the PD or MD, and whether the record was tested or added. If the station plays your record, the activity must be reported to the trades and the promoter should concentrate on stimulating upward chart movement.

Certain professionals within the independent promotion community specialize in niche marketing and other specialized tasks. These include coordinating promotional activities while a band is on tour, contests, and target mailings to special "fan lists."

THE ROAD TO THE CHARTS

Of course, fate and luck play a huge role in getting your music heard on the radio, but hard work is the biggest factor. If you decide that the DIY approach is for you, you will need to map out a meticulous strategy to get your music to the right station at the right time. If you just don't want to deal with record promotion, consider working with an independent promoter. It's their job to get your music heard.

CHAPTER 13

Surviving Club Gigs

If you're like most musicians that play club gigs, chances are you don't have access to luxuries like well-tuned sound systems, light shows, crystal-clear stage monitors, and sound checks. The reality of many small club gigs is coping with abused P.A. systems, indifferent house sound crews, and stages so tiny that you'll spend entire shows with the back of your legs rubbing against a kick drum and your left earlobe being rhythmically pulverized by the headstock of a Fender Precision. It's a sobering experience to realize that, for most musicians, the concert stage is not a tool to enhance one's performance, but a wicked patch of hell on earth.

Fortunately, there are ways to tame the savage club environment. If you just employ your creativity to think about more than chord changes, you *can* survive the travails of bringing your music out in the open.

GET ORGANIZED

The best protection against the frustrating anarchy of small clubs is scrupulous planning. Rehearse your act until it's second nature. Nothing is more annoying to an audience (or house sound person) than a band that diddles away onstage, apparently unaware of what to do next. Few of today's music fans—who have developed their attention spans experiencing the slam-bam presentation of MTV—have the patience to watch musicians struggle with ineptitude. You don't have to rigorously plan and choreograph every second of your show, but you should at least write out a set list to minimize onstage "down time."

Written documentation is extremely helpful when you're dealing with a house engineer. These much-maligned professionals are bombarded with inexperienced and unprofessional acts, and they often adopt devil-may-care attitudes as a survival tactic. Most of the time, by necessity, they just set up the mics and hope for the best. However, you can usually improve their demeanor by giving them two helpful sheets of paper.

A stage plot and a set list are invaluable tools if the sound person has never seen you perform. The stage plot instantly informs the sound person of the player's names, the instruments they play, and how they are arranged on stage. This guide is a tremendous help when something has to be tweaked in the middle of a set. For example, if a background vocal is buried in the mix, the sound person simply checks the stage plot for the singer's location and moves the appropriate fader. A house sound person will never make adjustments as quickly as someone who has rehearsed with the band, but the stage plot can certainly save an important harmony vocal from being lost for an entire song.

The set list is a professional courtesy because it gives the sound person a schedule of events. If a band starts to run over its allotted performance time, the sound person can instantly see how many songs are left in the set and signal for the act to cut one or two

A stage plot and a set list are
invaluable tools if the sound person has
never seen you perform.

The Club Gig Survival Kit

Below is a checklist of inexpensive items you shouldn't be without when you're on a gig. It may seem like a lot of things, but when gathered together they fit neatly into a small toolkit or sports bag. Don't forget to mark anything that could be confused with club equipment: DI boxes, extension cords, outlet boxes, microphone stands, mics, etc.

VOCALIST

- extra mic clips
- microphone
- mic cable
- mic stand

KEYBOARDIST

- adapter (three-prong to two-prong)
- direct box
- duct or gaffer's tape
- extra amp fuses
- extra audio cables
- extra MIDI cables
- extra power cables for instruments/mixer
- flashlight or penlight
- flat end screwdriver (normal size)
- flat end screwdriver (small tip)
- heavy duty extension cords (both three-prong and two-prong)
- multi-outlet boxes (with internal fuses)
- needle nose pliers
- Phillips head screwdriver (normal size)
- Phillips head screwdriver (small tip)
- pliers
- soldering iron/solder/sponge

GUITARIST/BASSIST

- adapter (three-prong to two-prong)
- direct box
- duct or gaffer's tape
- extra amp fuses
- extra power cable
- flashlight or penlight
- flat end screwdriver (normal size)
- flat end screwdriver (small tip)
- heavy duty extension cords (both three-prong and two-prong)
- long cables
- multi-outlet boxes (with internal fuses)
- needle nose pliers
- Phillips head screwdriver (normal size)
- Phillips head screwdriver (small tip)
- pliers
- short cables
- soldering iron/solder/sponge
- strings

DRUMMER

- cymbal stand parts (felts, plastic sleeves, wingnuts, etc.)
- drum keys
- drum lugs
- duct or gaffer's tape
- extra bass drum pedal
- extra hi-hat clutch
- extra snare and string or plastic strip (for attaching snare)
- extra snare drum
- rug (for wood/concrete floors)
- various heads

If you don't bring extras of every single thing that can break, blow up, or get lost, you're courting tragedy.

numbers. Granted it's always a drag to shorten your set, but a fair warning is preferable to the sound person's panic tactic of pulling the plug in the middle of a song.

HELLO OUT THERE

The stages of many clubs are architectural afterthoughts. For example, a bar owner who decides to offer live music might simply remove a few tables and cram a P.A. system near the restroom. But even club owners savvy to the requirements of live music can be hampered by the physical limitations of their venues.

A good percentage of small clubs are housed in former restaurants, warehouses, and storefronts. These spaces were not designed to accommodate large stages, lighting rigs, and concert sound systems. As a club owner wrestles to optimize audience sight lines and bar access, the bandstand often loses out to economic and space considerations. In other words, don't expect the classic rectangle shape that allows a well-positioned back line of amps facing the performers.

The necessity of fitting amps, drums, keyboard rigs, and band members into bizarre geometric configurations can make it difficult for performers to hear each other. You might find yourself on stages shaped like diamonds, triangles, L's, and circles, avoiding support beams, low-flying chandeliers, and onstage refrigerators. In tight situations, don't even try to set up a conventional back line. Position

amps on each side of the drum kit and angle them toward the center of the stage. This configuration immerses the drummer in the roar of the instruments and throws sound across the stage to the other band members. Obviously, the sound is not projected directly at the audience, but in a small club the rumble should punch through just fine. If you can raise the amps up on chairs or road cases, do so. Getting the speakers off the floor improves sound dispersal.

Hearing vocals onstage is another problem because club monitor systems are typically spartan and underpowered. Most of the time, you'll get two monitor wedges at the lip of the stage, but no monitor for the drummer (which is a big problem if your drummer sings). The only consistently workable way to fight a weak monitor system is to keep your instrument volumes down. If your stage volume is blasting, the house engineer will be unable to get the monitors loud enough to cut through the stage din. Period. Remember, there are live microphones up there, so feedback can be a problem if the monitor levels are too high. It doesn't pay to be stubborn because you can't win. If you want to hear yourself sing, turn down those amps! (And it's not a sin to ask your drummer to play softer, either.)

PEACE BY PIECE

Self-sufficiency is a good thing when you're dealing with the great unknown of club sound

A pair of work gloves will make carrying your gear on and off stage a touch easier on those invaluable musician's fingers.

systems. Never assume that the club can accommodate your needs: When in doubt, bring it yourself. Here are a few helpful hints developed from watching unprepared musicians self-destruct at gigs.

Vocalists. To ensure consistent sound quality, bring your own mic to each gig. Many clubs use Shure SM58s—which are great if your voice sounds good through one—but you'll encounter places where consumer-level microphones are the only option. But even if you adore SM58s, club mics can sound a bit ragged because they are sometimes dropped and abused by performers and inexperienced sound crews. Believe me, you'll be happier if you're singing through a known quantity. And don't forget to pack a handful of extra mic clips.

The selection of mic stands in most clubs is pretty limited, so I also recommend lugging your own boom stands to the show. If you play guitar or bass, straight stands make it difficult to "eat" the mic without banging your instrument against the stand. Obviously, keyboardists and drummers require a boom to extend the mic past their equipment.

Also, you should consider bringing your own mic cable. Most clubs don't have a large number of cables, and if the one they gave you starts making noise, it needs to be changed. Having your own as a back-up will save the sound person from having to hunt another one down, or worse, take one away from one of the instruments on stage. Don't forget to mark your cable, or get a brightly colored one, so it is easily identifiable as yours.

If you really want your vocals to shimmer, load up a small road rack with a compressor and multi-effects unit. Preprogram the signal processors to your favorite settings—although, you may have to tweak them when you start working with the club's acoustics—and carry the rack to the mixing station. Make sure that you have all the necessary connecting cables and that each cable is labeled ("compressor input," "compressor output," etc.). The sound person can simply patch your gear into the house mixing console to provide you with customized signal processing. Few sound crews will argue with having additional effects at their disposal, but it never hurts to call the club in advance of the show and inform them that you're bringing in an effects rack.

Guitarists and Bassists. For fretted performers, the operative word is "extra." If you don't bring extras of every single thing that can break, blow up, or get lost, you're courting tragedy. Make sure that your gig bag includes an additional power cord and fuses for your amp; spare guitar cables of assorted lengths; a handful of fresh 9V batteries for your stomp boxes and tuner; a backup guitar or bass; and a massive, almost inexhaustible supply of extra strings.

If you can, also bring guitar stands for each instrument, so you can readily grab a backup if a string breaks mid-song. Extension cords and multi-outlet boxes (with internal fuses) are also essential accessories because most stages never seem to have enough power

*The only workable way to fight
a weak monitor system is to keep your
instrument volumes down.*

outlets. Bass players should bring their own direct boxes.

Keyboardists. Frequent power fluctuations are an unfortunate fact of life in many clubs. If you want to protect your valuable gear, plug everything into a good AC line regulator to ensure stable AC. Bringing your own direct boxes can save frustration *and* fighting with your bass player over who gets the single direct box provided by the club. A cheap or used spare sound module should be standing by for emergencies. Also, label every input and output cable (audio *and* MIDI) to facilitate panic repatches if a module fails.

Drummers. Acoustic drummers should bring extra drum heads and a spare snare drum. If you break a snare, you can just reach for the spare and quickly exchange drums. Punctured tom heads are problematic because you can't take the time to remove and replace the head during a performance. However, covering the hole with a strip of gaffer's tape can keep you going until the break or end of the show. Like keyboardists, electronic drummers should bring spare cables and plug everything into a power conditioner. If you can afford a spare sound module, it never hurts to have a backup.

STRESS FIGHTERS

Performance jitters can also be minimized if you keep your mind engaged throughout the often numbingly boring process of setting up for the show. There's a lot of down time between loading and unloading gear, doing a sound check, and hitting the stage. Bring a book or some magazines to read during these numerous "hurry up and wait" periods. Also, you can diminish the nerve-wracking background noise of musicians chattering, bars being stocked, and other band's sound checks by wearing earplugs or listening to a portable cassette or CD player through headphones.

Getting food is sometimes an issue at clubs that are off the beaten path or in a city's industrial area. Even if a store or restaurant is within walking distance, a late sound check may not give you enough time to eat *and* prepare for the show. To avoid collapsing mid-set, always carry some crackers or another snack to stave off hunger until after the show. It's also smart to pack a bottle of water. Quenching thirst with booze or soft drinks can make you a bit woozy, especially on an empty stomach.

Unless you enjoy walking around drenched in sweat after a performance, a complete change of clothes, or at least an extra shirt , is advisable. Don't expect your "dressing room" (which is typically the club's bathroom) to have clean towels. Either bring your own, or plan to wipe your brow, neck, and hands with toilet paper. And speaking of hands, a pair of work gloves will make carrying your gear on and off stage a touch easier on those invaluable musician's fingers.

Bringing your own direct boxes can save frustration and fighting with your bass player over who gets the single direct box provided by the club.

To be completely honest, there will be those shows where careful planning won't save the day. When Fate tosses out one of her deadly curve balls, there's often nothing you can do except close your eyes and swing. But even if the stage is falling down around you, one psychic lifeboat is always available: your sense of humor. If, in the middle of a climatic solo, your keyboard rack explodes like the gluttonous diner in *Monty Python's The Meaning of Life,* brush the shrapnel from your hair and scat sing the final bars. A shrug and a chuckle always wins more audience support than visible panic.

CHAPTER 14

Showcasing for A&R

One of the most crucial steps toward getting a deal is performing at an industry showcase. It is the one time where having a high-powered lawyer, a mogul manager, and an ace producer will not make a bit of difference. Even a fabulous, self-produced CD can be a total waste if you can't play your music live when it counts. At a showcase, it's simply you and your music; play well, or lose the deal. Understanding the dynamics of the event will help you structure your showcase successfully.

Artist showcases are valuable to the industry and to the artists involved. Usually sponsored by performing rights societies or other musicians' organizations, these regional events show off the talents of the area's valuable music resources in a professional setting, stimulate and nurture the grassroots musical community, and provide a vehicle for music business professionals to work together and discover new talent.

WHY SHOWCASE?

Thanks to advanced music technology, many people can afford to produce their own masterpieces. However, record labels look at artists as investments, not art, so they want talented, appealing artists with long life-spans. To protect their sizable investment, they want a complete package: artists with great studio chops, charming personalities, immense stage charisma, and the ability to do the music-industry promotion game (meet and greets,

in-stores, special promotions, and so on) for several years.

Live-performance touring is not only a major sales tool for records, it's a means of "breaking" new bands, so it's absolutely necessary that a band be able to play. At showcases, the A&R reps get to know you and watch your development. It's also their first opportunity to bring more powerful label reps to see you. Your performance will determine whether you get signed, or need to go back and retool your act.

WHEN TO SHOWCASE

Bands should incorporate showcasing into their general business plan as part of their overall focused approach to developing industry relationships. A&R reps do not have time to keep coming to see you or wait for your act to develop. Remember, there are many thousands of bands trying to get signed. It is imperative that you make the most of your brief opportunity.

It's a mistake to showcase without a good demo because you don't have a good calling card to sustain interest in your band. It's also a huge mistake to showcase before you have your live show together. It's crucial to make a good impression on the reps; they go to a lot of these events, so they know how to spot the real deal. Focus on good song selection, good pacing of the set, and no dead stage time. This is not the time to fiddle with knobs or chat with each other. Play a short set of your

It's crucial to make a good impression
on the reps; they go to a lot of these events,
so they know how to spot the real deal.

best material; 20 to 35 minutes is long enough. Most reps make up their minds after the first three songs.

If the reps are interested, they will start to follow your live schedule, so don't just play one showcase and disappear. Make sure you have plenty of follow-up gigs. Make it easy for reps to see you by sending them notices with your gigs' correct start times. The most bothersome thing a band can do is advertise inaccurate start times; you don't want to make the rep cool his or her heels.

Sound and lights are important to your show, but only for your peace of mind. If you are happy with the staging, you will perform better. Most reps are more concerned about the essence of your presentation than its technical quality. They are looking for performance ability, personality, and stage presence. Of course, you don't want technical glitches that delay the show or break your rhythm, so make sure you have a thorough sound check to work out the bugs.

REGIONAL CONFERENCES

Regional music conferences and showcase weekends have become quite popular. These conferences aid the regional musical community and bring together all aspects of the music business.

Label reps take these weekends seriously; the prospect of checking out several bands at once is very attractive to them. The clubs take showcases seriously, too; they want to make a good impression on the reps as the proving ground for future hot up-and-coming acts. Therefore, many clubs upgrade their P.A. system and lights and make sure the showcase engineer is top-notch. This can help you put on a first-rate presentation.

Who gets selected to perform at these events is always subjective, and every conference planner has different criteria. There are a few basics that most planners share, though. First and foremost, a band must have a good demo. Production quality isn't as important as original songwriting, good singing, and solid playing, but with the affordability of pro-quality tools these days, there's no excuse for horrible production.

Second, the band should perform live and have a following. Crowd numbers aren't important; when a band plays off nights in clubs to establish a draw, they prove they are serious about their careers. Getting mentions in local press also shows they are working to get recognition. It doesn't matter how underground the press is, it's a start.

Finally, emerging management or attorney involvement is also a plus. While this is not absolutely necessary, it also shows that the band is committed to moving onto a more professional level.

Again, don't let the allure of major industry attention fool you into getting in over your head. It's too important of a career step to take lightly. Be patient and wait until you're ready.

CHAPTER 15

Booking Basics

When you add it all up, making music is a pretty tough gig. And I'm not just talking about the process of writing songs, putting together a band, rehearsing, and producing a demo. Once you've done all that, it's time to get out there and share the fruits of your labor with the public. The entertainment sections of local and regional papers list plenty of bands playing in all sorts of venues, but how can you go about getting these gigs? Well, there are a variety of ways to do this.

The most basic element of playing a gig is getting *booked,* which means that a club schedules you to play. Sounds simple enough, but here are some insights into how booking works and what you should do to increase your chances of getting booked for gigs, as well as a few tips to help you keep your sanity.

PLAN OF ATTACK

If you want to play the places best suited for your band, you're going to have to do some research and spend a good number of hours on the phone. Most clubs book local bands at least a month in advance, so it's best to start planning two to three months before you want to play.

In this chapter, we'll deal with booking locally or regionally—say, nothing more than an overnighter or a weekend trip away. (For information on putting together a tour, see chapter 16, "Planning and Booking a Tour.") If you are planning on going away for a night or two, you'll need to sort out some logistics, including what you need to bring, where you'll stay, food, transportation, gas costs, and so on. Come up with a ballpark figure so you won't be shocked if you find out your gigs might not even cover the costs involved in the trip.

There are a couple of ways to approach booking, and the smart musician will use both. One method is to try to hook up with other bands and see whether they can get you a slot as an opening act or refer you to the people who book the clubs where they've worked. Another way is to do your own research into all the possible places to play. Local newspapers and independent weeklies (e.g., *Village Voice, San Francisco Bay Guardian, L.A. Weekly*) are great sources of club information. Many even list all the clubs in the area, with phone numbers and addresses.

Target venues where your music fits in with the types of music the club generally books. Of course, if you're playing locally, you should be well enough tapped into your scene to know the venues that best suit your style of music. However, it never hurts to research the scenes in neighboring communities; you never know what you'll turn up.

Try surfing the Net for information on clubs. Most newspapers and weeklies, such as those mentioned above, have Web sites, and nightclubs often have their own sites as well as listings on city-oriented sites, such as City Search (www.citysearch.com) or Sidewalk (www.microsoft.com/sidewalk). A great place

As with most things in the music industry, your success in booking comes down to a few basic qualities: talent, reliability, and patience.

to check is the Club/Concert listing at the Ultimate Band List (www.ubl.com). This site has hundreds of club listings and links for venues all over the world, which makes it a good resource should you eventually decide to venture far outside your city limits.

In compiling your list of possible venues, don't forget to contact larger promoters; they often have opening slots to fill at bigger venues. Also, you might decide to take a gig in a larger place for less money—or even none— if you feel it would give you good exposure.

When you have narrowed down the list of places you really want to play, it's time to do a mailing and get their attention.

PUT THE WORD OUT

You don't need an extensive promotional package when you're looking to get booked. Gather photocopies of any significant press you've received and type out a short bio of your band. It's helpful to include photos to give bookers an idea of the band's aesthetic. Make sure your demo has the strongest material first. Bookers rarely have time to listen all the way through demos, so be sure your demo conveys the flavor of your band at the outset.

Also consider including something distinctive with your mailing, like a band sticker, a key chain, flyers, etc., that might keep your package from ending up at the bottom of a bin in someone's office. Put your demo and promotional materials together, add a short cover letter, and you're ready to roll.

LOG SERIOUS PHONE TIME

Once you've sent out your packages, you need to follow up with the booker at each club. Try your best to find out the club's "office hours" and call during that time. Bookers get hundreds of calls every week, and they only have so much time to return calls. So, be patient, call back after about three weeks, and expect a lot of busy signals. This is where your people skills are crucial. Remember that there is a fine line between staying on top of your business and being a relentless jerk; polite persistence usually pays off.

Keep your expectations realistic when it comes to the kind of gigs you'll get at first. You'll have to build a reputation in smaller clubs and play weeknight shows at the outset. Once you establish some sort of draw and develop a mailing list, you will have much more leverage with bookers.

Try to negotiate to get as much money as you can to cover your expenses. Bookers will offer you either a guarantee or a percentage of the money they make at the door. If it's a show out of town that is not paying much, ask whether the club can help you with accommodations or food. Some even have arrangements with local hotels or restaurants. But bear in mind that, when starting out, you might not make much money, if anything at all—especially in major music centers, such as Nashville, San Francisco, New York, and Los Angeles. Consider it an investment in your musical career.

Most clubs don't require a written contract, but it is best to have one on hand in case things go awry.

Another thing to keep in mind is that there is no surefire method of getting booked in a particular venue. Bookers have to think about the bottom line: how many paying people will you draw, and how much alcohol can the club sell? Bookers have different priorities when it comes to choosing live bands. Some want musicians to play quietly as background for dining, and some pride themselves on booking the talent of tomorrow. Take this into consideration before you set your heart on playing a particular venue.

GET IT IN WRITING

Once your hard work pays off and you have made an agreement, you should try to get it in writing. Most clubs don't require a written contract, but it is best to have one on hand and have it signed by the club in case things go awry. It doesn't have to be a complicated legal document; just outline the basic terms of the agreement: name and place of engagement, date of engagement, starting time, length of sets, and compensation.

Because most booking is done verbally, usually on the telephone, it is your responsibility to make sure that everyone involved is on the same page. When the inevitable misunderstandings occur, it is much better to have something in writing than to rely on the memory of others.

REEL THEM IN

Once you've booked some gigs, you need to promote them. The whole point of playing live is to get as many people out to the venue

Who Does What

booker   The person at a venue who schedules shows for the club. They listen to (many, many) demos and negotiate terms with bands.

booking agent   The person who books shows for bands. Most agents work for a percentage of what the band makes. They work independently or for an agency.

promoter   Promoters usually work on a regional basis and oversee all aspects of organizing a show or tour and promotion. Some promoters actually produce the show (get the venue, book the bands, supervise the evening's activities), and some are just responsible for promoting the show via print, radio, and street buzz.

stage manager   The person in charge of the logistics of the show. This generally includes the backstage area and getting the bands and equipment on and off the stage.

talent buyer   This term mainly refers to people who work for organizations that book for larger venues.

Keep your expectations realistic
when it comes to the kind of gigs
you'll get at first.

as possible, especially if it is in an area where you haven't played before. It's pointless to do all of the work to get booked just to play to an empty room. If the show goes well, it is more likely that the club will have you back again, and other clubs are more likely to book you if you have a good word-of-mouth reputation.

In short, do everything you can to fill the venue with bodies. Get together a mailing list, do in-store appearances, put up fliers around the city, set up interviews on local radio, or perform a free show at a college campus—whatever it takes to pack the house.

THE NEXT LEVEL

If you've been booking your own gigs for a while and are getting overwhelmed by sheer volume of work, you should consider using a booking agent. The type of agent or agency you should hook up with depends on the type of shows you're planning to do. Some agents only book certain types of venues or dates (e.g., clubs only or parties only), some just do regional booking, some only do national or international, and some do it all.

Usually an agent's fee is a negotiable percentage of the amount you will make for the show. If you don't make much money per show, you might have to pay your agent a flat monthly fee or take care of their expenses, such as mailings and phone bills. Many agencies work on the basis of exclusive agreements whereby they book all of your gigs. However, some agents, especially those who handle

local venues, can book you just for specific rooms. Occasionally, two or more agencies might even cooperate to help construct a tour—if the money is right.

Agencies understandably prefer to work with bands that can show a good track record of successful gigs at established venues, in addition to having a strong promotional package. If you are mostly interested in playing local and regional shows, booking through small agencies might be sufficient.

However, the ante goes up when you move to more extensive tours and bigger gigs. The larger, national booking agencies take several factors into account when considering new clients. These factors include radio airplay and record sales (even if they're just regional), along with a reputable label, lawyer, and manager. In general, a big agency wants to work with an act that has a good product and a good team in place.

That's not to say that you have to be booked by a major booking agency to achieve success at a regional or national level. As with most things in the music industry, your success in booking comes down to a few basic qualities: talent, reliability, and patience. Try to build a reputation as being not only musically talented but reliable when it comes to handling the business aspects of playing live. It'll get you a lot further than you might think.

CHAPTER 16

Planning and Booking a Tour

Planning and booking a tour requires more work than gassing up the van and stocking up on road maps. To make a tour successful, you'll need to deal with a lot of logistics and anticipate many situations before you leave home. And if you've never toured, even regionally, you're courting disaster if you try to set out without a game plan.

Following are some tips on how to go about formulating your tour plan and getting the dates secured. I'm assuming that at the very least your band has already created a demo of your material or, better yet, released a tape or CD, written a bio, and assembled a press kit.

ASSESSING THE SITUATION

Before you begin the actual booking process, make sure your band agrees upon all aspects of the tour. Avoid communication breakdowns by putting your final agreements in writing, which ensures that everyone has the same information. This helps circumvent nasty surprises like your keyboard player throwing a fit because you've planned to leave town before his softball season is over.

Once the departure date is set, you will have to stick to it, so get it right the first time. Nothing's worse than having to call back promoters who have given you a hold on a date to tell them that you'll actually be coming through town two weeks down the line. It can cost you some gigs and foul up your routing.

Geography lessons. Look at a map and decide which regions of the country you want to try to cover. It's imperative to calculate distances between your desired destinations to make sure you really can cover x amount of ground in y number of days. You'd be amazed at how many bands pile into their vans without even bringing along an atlas. If you already have a CD that's getting airplay on college or public radio stations, you'll have a huge head start; you can base your tour around cities where there's a chance that people have heard of you. Otherwise, you should base your decision around which areas are most likely to be responsive to your type of music.

Length of time on the road. Is everyone willing to take time off work for this endeavor or even quit their jobs? Is everyone in agreement that this should last for a week, two weeks, a month, or longer? The vacation or leave-of-absence arrangements must be made before you start setting dates. Of course, if you are a professional band, the tour *is* your job, but even so, you have to consider how long the band members can be away from home without destroying marriages, relationships, and so forth.

Workload. Determine the number of shows you will play per week and whether you want or need days off between shows for drive time or sightseeing. Obviously, when you're just starting out, you have to take what you can get, but make sure everyone is up to playing ten nights in a row or, conversely, is able

Once you've planned your route
and agreed upon the time frame,
the real work begins.

Musician Heal Thyself

Almost everyone gets sick on tour. Changing climates, hanging out in less-than-sanitary environments, meeting all kinds of people, and staying up too late are unavoidable situations. But you can try to keep a cold from turning into bronchitis or walking pneumonia by building up your immune system. Make sure you're in good physical health before you hit the road. Do all those common-sense things like eating well and getting plenty of exercise.

You should maintain your healthy habits on the tour, too. Drink plenty of water, try to take naps, and definitely get exercise when you can: bring a jump rope, skates, or a skateboard along; go running; bring a basketball; stop to swim in the summer; or take walks. Herbal and homeopathic medicines like echinacea and golden seal are becoming popular ways of strengthening the immune system. You might want to consider researching these types of options when putting together your tour "medicine kit."

Lastly, think ahead about what the weather will be like and pack accordingly: rain gear, wool socks, and warm hats are lifesavers, even in the summer, if you end up in the mountains at night.

to cool their heels for four or five days between the gigs you *can* get.

Of course, when you are cooling your heels, you are losing money. Part of booking a profitable tour is making sure you don't stay idle for long, so if you can't book enough dates to work steadily, maybe you should reconsider the whole tour. You might decide that the publicity you can get from a few key dates makes overall financial loss worthwhile, but if you make that choice, do so consciously, with your eyes open. You don't want infighting later on because some band members expected to make a monetary profit from a tour that was intended to be purely promotional.

Another aspect of figuring out workload

is how basic duties will be handled. Is everyone going to take turns driving? Who's going to handle the money, the loading and unloading of the vehicle, making phone calls? Perhaps it happens to work out that one person is great at accounting, another is mechanically inclined, another is good at selling merchandise, another is able to find his way effortlessly around cities he hadn't been in before, and another enjoys chatting up promoters. This type of job assigning might seem anal-retentive, but it makes touring smooth. It's up to you if you want to constantly get lost, show up late, carry your pay around in a paper bag that you keep losing in the van, or get stopped short by something as simple as a flat tire.

*One tactic is to start really early,
get one major show confirmed, and work
around that solid date.*

Financial survival. What if your guarantee falls through, or your 50-percent-of-the-door comes to $17 five shows in a row? Will you be able to spend your own money to feed yourselves, buy gas, and pay for repairs or even the occasional motel room? Hopefully, you have a band fund that can cover these expenses or are lucky enough to have at least one solvent member who can bankroll you through tough times. Credit cards, used judiciously, can be real lifesavers in these situations.

Gimme shelter. Figure out whether you can afford to stay in motels every night or are willing to sleep on strangers' floors or camp. Ask whether the club has a discount deal with a nearby motel or sets up accommodations for bands (e.g., a band house).

Everyone should have adequate bedding, just in case. Do all band members agree that it's okay to announce during your set that you need a place to sleep? It's a time-honored tradition that usually works out fine, but it's not particularly professional to solicit lodging from the stage. And it can lead you into some pretty odd or annoying situations—like all-night parties occurring right next to your sleeping bag.

Also, agree on food arrangements. Are you going to eat at fast food joints, truck stops, or cafes, or will you bring along a cooler (even a camp stove) and stock up at grocery stores along the way? If you are playing a club that serves food, you might be able to get a break on meals. Finding food on tour is tough for vegetarians, even these days, and it can be extremely difficult for those on macrobiotic or special diets. Plan accordingly and bring what you need. Check your local bookstores for guides to vegetarian restaurants across the country.

Think about how many other people, if any, you will bring along. Can you afford to bring a roadie, sound person, or someone who can sell merchandise for you? Or is having extra space in the van more desirable? It's also important to agree beforehand whether significant others can come along. (Remember what happened in *This is Spinal Tap*?) Your vehicle is your home on wheels, and if you've only read about "group dynamics" in Psychology 101, now you'll experience it firsthand. Try not to become a dysfunctional family.

FINDING THE GIGS

Once you've planned your route and agreed upon the time frame, the real work begins. Considering that there are way more bands than venues, how do you get the attention of clubs across the country?

Your first task is to find out where the clubs are and how to contact them, which can be a frustrating task for beginners (see chapter 15, "Booking Basics"). Many resources are available to help you with your venue search, such as regional newspapers for the areas you plan to visit, books, and magazines like *Pollstar* and even that punk mainstay *Maximum RockNRoll*. Every month *CMJ* (*College Music Journal*) does a city scene report that lists

*Part of booking a profitable
tour is making sure you don't
stay idle for long.*

everything of interest to touring bands, along with phone numbers. Get a hold of back issues and use them!

You can also try calling college radio stations. (Obviously, this works best if they already have your music and like it.) If they aren't inundated with calls, music directors and DJs may be able to tell you which clubs might actually take your calls, which ones should be avoided, and whether there are "alternative," non-nightclub venues such as warehouses, storefronts, record stores, theaters, college organizations, large book/music stores (e.g., Borders Books), coffee houses, or even private houses.

Search on the Internet for each city you'd like to play. You'll often find listings for all sorts of venues for each genre of music, along with reviews of the clubs or various scenes. Keep in mind that this information will be opinionated and possibly in need of updating. Even lurking around in music-related chat rooms may uncover some leads.

If you are acquainted with a band who has gone on the road, pump them for their contacts. Most people are willing to share information. Go to your local club and approach touring bands who seem similar to yours and are just slightly above your level of recognition. Don't bother talking to bands who play huge venues because that's probably out of your league at this point.

Assemble a list of potential clubs in each city you hope to visit. Make calls before you send anything so you'll know whether your music fits into the club's format. Also, find out which nights they feature live music. The worst thing you can do is to send off a promo kit without knowing anything about the club. Some promoters might be kind enough to refer bands to more appropriate clubs, but don't expect it. You have to do your homework.

When you have tracked down a venue that looks promising, *then* send the tape, remembering to put your name and phone number on everything. Make sure you budget for postage costs, which can add up quickly. Is it worth it to send your packages via UPS, or do you want to use registered or First Class mail? You should begin this process at least three and a half months before you hope to start the tour. Many promoters start filling in their calendars two or more months in advance, and these are minimum estimates.

RATIONAL ROUTING

Get a calendar with plenty of room for scrawling, and pencil in your tentative route. When you start making calls, your routing should be fairly loose; don't say you're only available on October 15. You're more likely to get a show if you give promoters a window of opportunity. Tell them you're looking for something in the October 13 to 16 range. This part can be tricky. It's about strategy. One tactic is to start really early, get one major show confirmed, and work around that solid date.

Before getting on the phone, consider

When planning your tour budget,
you should factor in the costs of fixing, maintaining,
and even customizing your vehicle.

alternate scenarios you can fall back on if your ideal routing isn't panning out. You may end up having to drive more than you'd prefer: for example, going from Minneapolis to Ann Arbor and then backtracking to Chicago. Always keep your atlas handy so you'll know if it's physically possible to zigzag from one city to another in a few days. First tours often involve driving in triangles rather than perfect linearity.

PHONE TAG: YOU'RE IT!

You'll spend a lot of money on long distance phone calls. It can take a dozen calls to solidify one gig. Promoters are swamped with tapes and press kits and often won't return calls, especially to unknowns. It's imperative to be persistent, professional, and genuinely friendly. If you leave accusatory, whining, "why won't you call me" messages on their voice mail, you're *never* going to hear from them. This is where that anal-retentive job-assigning comes in handy: make sure the band member with the best phone skills is the one making the calls. Promoters and bookers hate dealing with musicians who are unintelligible and not concise. Their time is precious, and you don't win points if you waste it.

You will run into promoters who say they never got your package. Be prepared to send out replacement packs via priority mail. You must try to determine whether these talent buyers are lying to you. If they brush you off a third time, saying the tape never arrived or

was "lost," it may be their way of bowing out. If you think this may be the case, it can't hurt to ask them point blank. You should also ask them if there's another venue that might be more open to your music.

You must keep an organized, detailed log of all this. In addition to the calendar, get a durable notebook, electronic organizer, or laptop computer (depending on your budget), and make notes about each call. For example, *7/18: Bob hasn't listened to tape yet, says to call back in 2 days. 7/20: He listened to tape but sounds unsure about what kind of bill we'd work on. I suggested blah blah blah....Call back early next week.*

NAILING THE DATE

If bookers seem to be waffling, you have to convince them that your band is worth a risk. If you know any bands in a particular area that are willing to vouch for you, now is the time to call in favors.

There's also the type of booker who does not listen closely to your tape. They may put it on, then become distracted with calls and not know what they heard. You should be prepared to describe your music and appeal over the phone. This can be abhorrent, but sometimes they need to hear you compare yourself to a band they're familiar with. Think like a music critic and tell them you are somewhere between x and z. Tell them exactly what bands you'd be a perfect opener for and why, but go easy with the hard sell. They get that all day

Some clubs actually have a policy that allows them to kick a band off the bill if they show up after sound-check hours are officially over.

long from professional booking agencies who have the rosters to back it up. Pro booking agencies sometimes force venues to take on one of their unknown acts before the venue is "allowed" to host a well-known sure bet. You don't have that kind of leverage.

If the booker still sounds unsure, you must decide whether this particular gig is worth playing for "gas money" or even for free. (Remember, you should keep your expectations realistic when it comes to how much money you'll be making.) Bands that bring lots of tapes, CDs, cool-looking T-shirts, and other "product" will often take these kinds of shows, knowing that if luck is on their side, they can sell enough merchandise after their set to get to the next town *and* keep themselves fed.

While on the road, you'll probably get tips about venues that are open to trying out new acts. It might be worthwhile to cancel a scheduled day off in favor of driving all day to make that extra show. It's also helpful to leave yourself open to end-of-tour possibilities. Any such tips you receive should go right into your tour notebook. Don't count on remembering what a number scrawled on a matchbook means.

CONTRACTS

You might wonder whether promoters would take contracts from unknown, "unrepresented" bands seriously. It doesn't hurt to put together a simple, 1-page contract that lists your band name, date of show, and how much

of a guarantee or percentage of the door you discussed with the club, and leave a space for the official signature of the booker. For the hell of it, consider including a few lines about a food buy-out and some free beer.

This will often work pretty well for you. It doesn't hurt to ask for these things, as long as you are low-key and don't come off like you expect royal treatment. The clincher is to get the booker to sign and return the contract (send it with an SASE) before you leave for the tour so you can use it as proof that someone really agreed to pay you.

For the most part, I have assumed that you are the average band making a go of it with very little in the way of connections. However, if you are a local union band, the situation is a bit different. For a start, you must use a standard union contract, and you get a certain level of protection against contract breaches. You also can take advantage of the Musicians Union's (800) ROADGIG emergency phone line if you run into trouble on the road or at venues. Some union locals have services that help you with booking, and agencies that book union acts might advertise for bands in your local union paper or in the *International Musician*.

ADVANCING THE DATES

No matter what, you must call the promoter and verify that you really are booked for the date and that everything is in order. Do this at least twice before the show: once a couple

*Make sure the band member
with the best phone skills is the
one making the calls.*

The Band Van

If you have played locally for a while, you probably have a van or other large, gear-lugging vehicle. Make sure it's up to the rigors of hauling you, your bandmates, and your gear from town to town. It's more than a vehicle; it'll be your home, office, and storage facility for the duration of your tour.

When planning your tour budget, you should factor in the costs of fixing, maintaining, and even customizing your vehicle. You'll certainly want new tires and a full tune-up, and you'll have to have any existing problems repaired. You might want to make special upgrades such as building a loft or a secure equipment-storage box. Also, if you don't have it already, you should get emergency road-service coverage (e.g., AAA's Plus package).

Here are some must-have items when outfitting your vehicle for a tour: spare tire; heavy-duty hydraulic jack; tool box; flashlight and batteries; rags; large, unbreakable water container; chains and padlocks to keep spare tire and battery from being ripped off; plenty of strong rope; tire chains, if you are going into snow country; cooler; crates for all the junk you'll acquire along the way; garbage bags; reading light; atlas; city maps; and last, but not least, the indispensable Swiss Army knife. If you plan to tour for extended periods, you also would do well to have a CB radio so you can monitor road conditions and get help in an emergency. Cell phones are de rigeur for traveling salespeople nowadays, and they're handy for bands, too, if you can afford them.

Taking two or more vehicles considerably increases your overhead, but it also increases your payload and flexibility. And it keeps the band at least partially mobile if one vehicle breaks down. If you do travel in tandem, it's important to develop car-caravan skills; just for starters, stay fairly close together (preferably in visual range), with the slowest vehicle in the lead. CB radios or cell phones are especially handy in this scenario for communications between vehicles. Tow chains and ropes come in handy if you are caught in the middle of nowhere and have to tow a crippled vehicle to the nearest shop.

weeks before and once two to three days before. If you're not traveling with a sound person, this is the time to make sure that the venue has someone available to do sound.

Find out exactly when they expect you to load in, when sound check is, and what your set lengths and times will be. Don't forget to ask whether the schedule is based on real time or bar time. (Many clubs set their clocks ten or fifteen minutes ahead to allow a margin of safety for clearing everyone out at closing time.)

Make sure you ask the promoter for all possible numbers for the club. Sometimes

When you first show up, you need to find the promoter, introduce yourself, and ask who settles up at closing time.

there's a direct line that people will answer all the time and another line where voice mail kicks in after office hours. Get the promoter or stage manager's home number, as well. Remember that durable notebook or laptop you used for booking the tour? Bring it along on tour and continue to make notes, write down directions and all phone numbers, and definitely include your impressions of how the actual gig went. (For example, did the sound person show up? Did the monitors work? Were you paid fairly? Did they give you great food for free?) This will be a great reference tool for future tours.

If the promoter's not there, get directions from the bartender or whomever answers the phone. Ask when the sound person normally shows up. In fact, ask *exactly* what time the club opens and when the sound person *really* shows up. Clubs often take the offensive and tell bands to show up at 4 P.M., even though the place doesn't open until 5 P.M. and the sound person never gets there before 6 P.M. They just assume bands will be late.

If one day you *are* running late—you got lost, had a flat tire, or your drummer and bass player took off walking to a thrift store that's two miles away ten minutes before you were supposed to leave town—it's in your best interest to call ahead. That way they know you're still coming and can reschedule or cancel your sound check. In addition, the sound person gets to go eat dinner instead of waiting around for you to show up. Be assured, if you make Spike wait, he will punish you later.

Some clubs actually have a policy that allows them to kick a band off the bill if they show up after sound-check hours are officially over.

A TRUE HORROR STORY

A friend's band was out on their first tour, and they didn't advance their shows. They drove from Lubbock, Texas, to Oklahoma City only to find out that the club where they were supposed to play had changed owners and was now a dance club. The slimy promoter hadn't bothered to call the acts he had booked before he skipped town. Their next show was in Albuquerque. They had driven for hours, basically in the opposite direction of their next show, for nothing. This could have been avoided with a couple of quick phone calls.

Advancing shows on the road means that practically every time you stop for gas somebody has to be on the phone calling ahead to the next two or three clubs or promoters in order to verify load-in and sound-check times and get directions to the club. It might work for band members to take turns doing this at each stop so that everyone has a chance to wander around the truck stop, play Frisbee, or call their sweetie. Or maybe just one of you is best at this task. Whatever the case, just make sure it gets done.

GETTING PAID

Somebody in your band has to keep it together enough to remember to track down

It's also helpful to leave yourself open to end-of-tour possibilities.

the promoter and get paid. Promoters can be very elusive at the end of a long night, and unscrupulous ones will just go home or have the bartender lie and say they can't find them. That's why, when you first show up, you need to find the promoter, introduce yourself, and ask who settles up at closing time.

While we're on the subject of money, beware the road-band treasurer's hidden enemy: the bar tab. You don't want to get to the end of a week-long run at a club and find out that the drummer and lead singer ran up huge bar and restaurant tabs that are being deducted from the band's pay. For this reason, some band leaders have a hard pay-as-you-go rule, regardless of whether the bar is willing to allow tabs. At any rate, make sure the band rules are clear on this matter at the outset, and if you do allow tabs, keep track of them so that the bills don't exceed the musicians' ability to pay.

HIT THE ROAD, JACK

It's the potential payoff for all this planning and hard work that makes the endeavor worthwhile. If you plan it right (and roll with the inevitable problems you *didn't* plan on), you can gain new friends and fans all across the country. Also, if your band can survive all that togetherness, you've learned yet another survival tool on your road to success in the music business.

3

Taking Care of Business

**Personal Career Advice for
Musicians, from Running Your Own
Studio to Financing Your Band**

CHAPTER 17

Insuring Your Gear

Far too many musicians don't insure their equipment. Most think they can't afford it. Some think their gear is too old to be worth insuring. Still others want to get equipment insurance, but aren't sure where to start. None of these excuses is valid. First of all, if you have a sizable investment in your equipment, it's probably worth protecting with insurance. Even if it's old, it will still cost a lot to replace it, and insurance companies will reimburse policy holders for the replacement cost of their gear, not the street value. Lastly, most companies that offer homeowner's or renter's insurance will insure your gear.

SPIN THE WHEEL

Insurance is a classic betting game. Some people think they can beat the odds and avoid disaster, but as with most gambling, they're betting on something they can't control. Can you be sure that your upstairs neighbor won't fall asleep with a cigarette in his hand and burn down your building? Is your band's van full of equipment really safe for just ten minutes parked in the alley behind the club? A colleague relates the story of a roadie for a rock band who kept the band's instruments in his garage *for one night*. Guess what? The next morning there was an empty garage and an unemployed roadie.

And it's not just human nature you have to guard against; Mother Nature can also inflict her share of damage through floods, earthquakes, hurricanes, and tornadoes. If you have even a modest investment in your equipment, or you play out, thus exposing yourself to more risk, you should investigate a few of the insurance options open to you.

Most insurance companies offer special riders to homeowner's and renter's policies to cover special items of any kind, not just musical equipment. Some policies even cover gear that is stolen or damaged outside of your place of residence. Also, many professional organizations offer musical-equipment insurance policies. In general, such group plans have better rates than individual ones because they are cheaper to administer and the risk is spread over a larger population.

THE BENEFITS OF BELONGING

As mentioned above, if you are a member of a professional service organization, a performing rights society, or the American Federation of Musicians (AF of M), you probably are eligible for a variety of services, including health and disability insurance, credit union, job listings, and equipment insurance.

Most of the gear insurance plans offered by these types of organizations are "all risks" policies, meaning that policy holders are covered worldwide, whether at home, at a gig, or on the road. This type of coverage includes theft from a locked vehicle, fire, natural disaster, and physical damage. Instances that are not covered include wear and tear (i.e., standard deterioration), theft from an unlocked

Whatever type of insurance you choose,
you should keep an impeccable record
of your equipment.

vehicle, and war and nuclear explosion.

As with any legal agreement, these policies have a few particulars. For individual items valued at, for example, $10,000 or more, you might be required to submit a bill of sale or a written appraisal before the item can be added to your policy. (The actual price point will vary depending on the plan.) Also, policy holders are responsible for providing the insurance company with specific records and information (see the "Details" section below for a list).

Again, the plans vary depending upon the specific policy offered through the organization. For example, the AF of M policy includes DJ and karaoke equipment, and the ASCAP policy covers computers and software. If you are a member of any of these types of organizations, contact them to learn about the options available to you.

ON YOUR OWN

If you don't belong to a special musician's organization, you still have insurance options, mostly through homeowner's or renter's insurance. In most cases, musical equipment is covered under a separate rate for "scheduled properties." Such properties are specifically itemized possessions that don't normally fit within the confines of a standard homeowner's insurance policy. Don't assume that just because you have homeowner's insurance that your gear is covered; be sure to check with your agent.

Most homeowner's policies don't limit the amount of equipment you can insure, but if there is a large investment in equipment, especially if it is used professionally, a rider is required. The rates also vary depending on how much equipment you insure and whether you are insured as an amateur or a professional. If you operate your home studio as a commercial enterprise, it probably won't be covered under homeowner's insurance, even with a separate rider. You'll most likely need insurance through the commercial division of your insurance company.

In fact, ask the insurance carrier if it is possible to "schedule" equipment with a rider regardless of how much you have. With such a rider, the equipment will be covered for a wider range of perils than under a standard policy. With some plans, equipment insured as scheduled properties is insured for loss outside the home. Also note, though, that such items are only covered if out of the home temporarily, not if permanently stored elsewhere. Another benefit of scheduling items is that you can choose to insure your equipment at replacement cost because you tell the insurance company how much insurance you want. And as mentioned above, most homeowners' and renters' policies require a written appraisal for items valued at $10,000 or more.

DETAILS

Whatever type of insurance you choose, you should keep an impeccable record of your

*Don't assume that just because
you have homeowner's insurance that
your gear is covered.*

equipment. Your insurance company will give you a specific list of the paperwork they need from you, but the following tips should help you get started.

Documentation. Record the name, model, and serial number of each piece of equipment. Once insured, new equipment purchases must be reported within a specified time period; check with your agent for your policy specifications. Also, if you need to file a claim because of theft, your insurance company will probably require a police report.

Photos and receipts. Store individual color photos or video of each piece of gear, bills of sale, and appraisals in a safe place. You may want to consider storing them in a safe-deposit box. If a fire, flood, or earthquake gets your gear, chances are it will get all of your paperwork, too.

Appraisals. If you don't have a bill of sale for some of your equipment, get a written appraisal. An appraisal is also necessary if you want to insure your gear at replacement value rather than at the cost you paid for it.

NOW WHAT?

I won't tell you that evaluating and choosing a plan then getting the paperwork together isn't a hassle, but it is worth it. The time and money you spend now will pay off the next time Mother Nature decides to flex her muscles, at the expense of your roof and everything under it.

CHAPTER 18

When Your Studio Goes Pro

I t's finally happening. You're actually making money recording and producing music from your home studio, and word is out on the street that you can be counted on to turn out killer demos or multimedia soundtracks. Whatever your specialty, it's clear that your home studio is growing up; it's becoming a full-fledged, income-generating studio. And that means you've lost your amateur status.

Once you decide to operate your home studio for profit, life becomes more complicated. It's not enough to be a musical genius, you have to possess a little business savvy, too. Ignoring certain business realities can lead to serious consequences, from lawsuits to IRS audits. By checking out a few basic laws and using some common sense, you can reap the rewards of being your own boss and doing what you enjoy: making music.

GETTING DOWN TO BUSINESS

The first step in setting up your project studio as a business is filing a fictitious business-name statement with your city clerk. Not only does this legally establish your studio as a business entity, it gives you the credibility and perceived stability of being a "real company," rather than "Joe Blow, Musician at Large." The filing requirements vary from city to city, but you'll most likely need to publish a public notice in a local newspaper stating your business name.

You should also obtain a trademark or servicemark for your company name. These may be established at the local, state, national, and international levels. If you want to break into the national music market, you should get a federal trademark. That way, you'll know if someone else is already using the name at a national level, which beats having to change it once you've already built up a reputation under that name.

Be forewarned that if you intend to use your project studio to produce band projects, the increased (and perhaps constant) flow of people may alert neighbors that a commercial business is in operation. If your residential area is not zoned for commercial use, you could be shut down or refused a business license. Be sure to check into your local zoning ordinances. But even if zoning isn't a concern, you should always consider your neighbors and your neighborhood when setting up your studio. If you have musicians and clients showing up at your door at all hours, the neighbors might not be understanding. Avoid scheduling sessions early or late in the day, when increased noise and traffic is most annoying. Incurring the wrath of your neighbors could mean more than some social unpleasantness; they could unleash the city hall hounds on you for noise pollution or for causing a public nuisance.

However, if you plan to work alone producing works for hire—such as film scores, multimedia soundtracks, or advertising jingles—you shouldn't encounter any zoning problems. Maintaining your project studio as a solo venture is no different than graphic

Be sure you know the terms
of payment before you start
on a project.

artists who design ads and brochures from their living rooms.

Other business basics include filing for your federal tax identification number and establishing a bank account under your business name. (If you plan to run your studio as a sole-proprietorship, you won't need a federal tax ID number. Your social security number will suffice.) With this paperwork out of the way, clients can make payments directly to your business name, which makes the IRS happy when it comes time for you to declare your business income.

THE TAXMAN COMETH

One of the benefits of establishing your personal studio as a business is that you can write off equipment purchases and depreciation, as well as other "reasonable and necessary" expenses. A few misguided souls believe that they can take some of their income under the table and still write off hefty business expenses. The IRS is always on the lookout for such shenanigans, so keep it above board. Also, be sure to play fair with what you define as reasonable and necessary. You can't deduct the cost of a Ferrari because you need it for your image. Reasonable and necessary for a studio would be things like gear, tape costs, repairs, and so on.

The IRS has recently cracked down on the home-office deduction. You are allowed a deduction for the percentage of rent/mortgage that your studio takes up in your home,

but only if the space is used exclusively for that purpose. For example, if your studio takes up 25 percent of your living space, you can deduct 25 percent of your house payment as a business expense. However, if your studio is in your living room and you watch TV and eat dinner in there, you are not eligible to take the deduction.

If you're not sure what you can and cannot declare, consult a tax attorney or an accountant. He or she can also advise you on issues such as paying employees should you hire any, taking on partners, and other legal subtleties of owning a business.

PLAYING THE ODDS

Equipment insurance is a must for all musicians, even those with relatively modest setups. The "It Won't Happen to Me" attitude is for suckers; you never know when an act of Mother Nature or human nature will conspire against you. (See chapter 17, "Insuring Your Gear.")

Furthermore, if you have session players, clients, or employees coming in to your studio, consider getting liability insurance. You want to be covered should a visitor get hurt on your property or if a neighbor's property is damaged by someone working in your studio. Your homeowner's or renter's policy may not cover business-related claims, so check your current policy carefully and add any necessary liability riders, or take out a separate policy.

Learn to do as much
of the maintenance as
possible by yourself.

MONEY MATTERS

An important part of running a successful business is handling money matters intelligently. The most basic issue is what to charge your clients. It's pretty easy to ascertain the going rate in your area for specific services, especially things like song demos and radio jingles: just ask your friendly competitors what *they* charge, or ask local bands, songwriters, and businesses what they usually pay for these services. Keep in mind that your clients will have different budgets and, consequently, different expectations as to what their money is buying them. If you're not sure what to charge for a job, get a price range from your client before committing yourself to a rate that is ridiculously low or prohibitively high.

One studio owner, who asked to remain anonymous, learned this technique the hard way. "When I started out, I was used to working with really small budgets," he says. "A car manufacturer contacted me about doing an advertising score. They explained what they needed and asked how much I charged. I thought I could do it for $4,000 or $5,000, but I decided to be brave and double it. I ended up asking for $9,000. They just looked at me and said, 'Well, if you can do a good job for $9,000, maybe you could do a *great* job for about $30,000.' I felt like such an idiot. From that point on, I learned to let the clients name their price ranges, and then I lay out what I can do for them based on what they can afford."

Other money issues concern keeping track of what you spend and what is owed to you by your clients. Many personal studio owners rely on generating their own invoices for services rendered. If you're not confident of your accounting abilities, software programs are available to help you out. The most basic way to track invoices is to use simple spreadsheet programs such as those in Microsoft's *Excel*, *Lotus 123* from Lotus Development Corp., or Claris' *ClarisWorks*.

Musicians making the transition to studio owners are often surprised at how long it can take to get paid, especially when dealing with larger companies. Some advertising agencies and record companies pay vendors on a 60-, 90- or even a 120-day billing period. This especially hurts when you're first starting out; you have to expend some cash to get up and running and then you have to wait a few more months before the money starts coming in.

Be sure you know the terms of payment before you start on a project. By keeping diligent client records, you can manage your money and know when to call a client if payment seems to be taking a long time to arrive. It's not unreasonable to ask for a percentage of your fee up front, but don't expect it. Also, don't be shy about calling a client after 60 days to check on the status of your payment. You don't want to develop a reputation as a person who is constantly pestering clients for money, but you don't want to be a sucker either. So use your judgment as to when to make follow-up calls, and always behave in a professional manner.

*If you're not sure what you can
and cannot declare, consult a tax attorney
or an accountant.*

DETAILS, DETAILS

As important as it is to keep a handle on major issues such as taxation, don't forget about the day-to-day matters involved in running your studio. Equipment maintenance is vital. You can't afford to have your machines breaking down when you need them most. Learn all you can about your gear and clean it regularly to prevent down time.

If you can, learn to do as much of the maintenance as possible by yourself. You benefit by saving money on repairs and by being able to do repairs on the spot, rather than waiting hours, days, or weeks for a technician to do it.

You should also pay attention to your studio's appearance. Invest in a couple of decent chairs, some end tables, and a nice lamp or two. Most ad execs will be less than pleased if they have to sit on overturned milk crates and risk soiling their Armani suits. Remember, you're running a business now, so you want your studio to be comfortable and inviting, not a dirty mess. You might also find that you are more productive if your workplace is clean and organized.

Your home's appearance is important, too, especially if clients have to walk through your living room and past the kitchen to get to the studio. Smelly laundry and a bathroom that looks like a science experiment gone awry are not the best ways to impress your clients.

Make no mistake about it, running your own studio is no picnic. But the rewards are many. Not only do you get to make music for a living, but you can choose projects that interest you while working in the comfort of your own home. You'll save yourself a lot of tears and gray hairs by understanding the rules of the game *before* you play.

CHAPTER 19

Financing Your Band

There is just one thing missing from your band's master plan. You have good songs and a decent following, but all you need is money. Money for equipment, studio time, a professional-looking promotional package…the list is endless. Unfortunately, your resources are tapped out and stardom cannot wait a second longer. Fret not, the solution to your dilemma lies in an understanding of financing techniques.

A number of basic financing vehicles are available for your project and career. Many musicians tend to mistakenly lump "money people" into two general categories: evil people who merely wish to exploit musicians like any other commodity and benefactors looking for a write-off instead of a pay-off. If you are seeking third-party financing, these misconceptions will certainly prevent you from hammering out a viable financing scheme.

Third-party financing is simply trading something of value that you have (the ability to create intellectual property, such as a record or songs, which eventually leads to money in the form of future royalties) in exchange for immediate cash. Financing can come in a number of forms, all being variations of this "fair trade" theme.

FINANCE STRATEGIES

Prior to seeking third-party financing, you need to understand the distinction between financing a project and financing your career.

Don't let the lure of ready cash tempt you into ignoring or overlooking this distinction because it could affect your career forever.

When making a deal to finance a *project,* the boundaries of the investors' involvement are finite. It is crucial for you to identify exactly what the project is (a recording project, a video, equipment for your studio, a showcase, a number of specific songs, etc.). Detailing your project in this way works well for both parties: the investor has a clear idea of how much money will be spent over a given period of time, and you have a clear idea of what royalties the investor will participate in.

On the other hand, when an investor puts up money for your *career,* it could result in infinite investor participation. For example, what if an investor pays for a demo project in exchange for a percentage of all of your future earnings in the entertainment industry? If you were to embark on a 15-year cash-producing binge as a recording artist, songwriter, and movie star, a piece of the millions of dollars you generate is a monetary return far in excess of the relatively small sum the investor put up for the demo recording. Newspapers and courtrooms are filled with stories of parties who at one time supported an artist in the early days in exchange for "a piece of the pie when they made it."

Let's look at a number of possible financing scenarios.

The money for financing a creative project usually comes from the Three Fs: family, friends, and fans.

Investors Gone Awry: A Cautionary Tale

The Capital Investments, a fictitious rock band, put the word out on the street that they were looking for cash to finance their demo project. Along came Joe Dolarz, a long-time fan of the band who told them he would lend them $5,000 for the project that "you guys can pay back when you finish the demo." The band bought some new equipment with the money but were once again strapped for cash for the studio time.

Another investor, Bigg Bux, offered to "pick up the recording tab" in exchange for "a couple of points from the outcome of the project." Bux also expended $5,000—enough to track five songs, but only to mix three. In the interim, it looked like the project had come to an end and Dolarz needed his money back, so he asked for the return of his $5,000 with interest. Rather than sell the equipment they purchased, the band signed a document prepared by Dolarz that granted him "repayment of his $5,000 with interest and a 20 percent partnership interest in the Capital Investments when the group made it big."

The band hit the streets again and made yet another deal, this time with Amy Investor, who paid for the mixing of the final two tracks and the pressing of a CD. She also agreed to have a few of her movie-industry friends listen to the album in exchange for "the copyright in the masters, the songs on the masters, and all income generated from those copyrights." Amy's cash outlay was $10,000.

The CD was released and ended up as half of a multimillion-selling soundtrack for a major motion picture. The Capital Investments signed a record deal with a major label, as well as a movie contract about their

DEBT FINANCING

Any way you cut it, you need to pay back a loan. Debt financing, or a loan, can come in many forms: charging your project on a credit card, a personal loan from a financial institution such as a bank or credit union, or signing a promissory note with a private party for a specified sum of money. All of these types of loans have a specific dollar figure that is invested, a specific time when it is to be paid back, and, usually, a specific interest rate for the "use" of the money. Collateral, such as equipment, is often pledged to secure the debt. Should the money not be repaid, the collateral may be sold to repay the debt.

The up side is that once the loan is paid off, your obligation to the lender is over; no looking over your shoulder should you make it to the big time. The possible down side is the project may not take off in relationship to the money borrowed and you may be saddled with a sizable debt to pay off.

*The more detailed your financial
relationship the fewer problems you may run
into when royalties start to flow.*

rags-to-riches story. All of the investors came to visit the Capital Investments as they were sunbathing in Maui to celebrate their success. Here is the outcome:

Dolarz expectations. Dolarz now feels that the interest on his loan should be 20 percent and that he is entitled to his 20 percent interest as a partner in the group because, "If it weren't for me, they couldn't have made the recordings that made them big." In addition, as a partner, Dolarz has started a campaign to fire the group's drummer. ("His image is all wrong," maintains Dolarz.) Dolarz is now in court seeking enforcement of his contract with the band.

Bux's expectations. Bux feels that all of the group's success is an "outcome of the project" and therefore he should be paid a percentage of their gross earnings. Being a "good guy," Bux has offered not to hassle the group in court if they give him an executive producer royalty of 5 percent of the movie soundtrack and 10 percent of the publishing revenue from the songs on the record.

Investor's expectations. Investor is seeking all royalties generated from the sales of the records and songs made famous by the soundtrack. With a now-successful publishing catalog, Investor was able to negotiate a several hundred-thousand dollar copublishing deal with a major music-publishing company, allowing her to sign other writers and songs to her new venture.

What the Capital Investments believed. The Capital Investments were simply trying to finish a project. They gave away pieces of the pie in exchange for cash and ended up giving away more than they could make, as well as taking on partners they didn't anticipate having.

EQUITY FINANCING

Taking on financial allies to further your career can be a blessing or a curse. In many states, two types of partnerships—general and limited—are available for your project or career. In a general partnership, all partners participate in the management and control of the business venture. The limited partnership, on the other hand, requires a general partner who will manage the business and one or more limited partner(s) who participate only on the money level. Limited part-

ners, then, do not participate on the management side and are liable only to the extent of their investment.

No matter how great the benefits of a general partnership may seem, think carefully before jumping in. Putting a person with business savvy on your team while you handle the creative aspects might sound tempting, but the skills and leadership that led this partner to success in his or her field might not translate well to the music business. Also keep in mind that this partner would have an equal say in the management aspects of your career,

In a general partnership,
all partners participate in the management
and control of the business venture.

which could cause problems if he or she isn't familiar with the music industry. ("Hey, mind if I tag along and make comments while you mix your record? I'm only protecting my investment, partner.")

A variation of the partnership form of investment is the joint venture, which is very much like a partnership but has a more narrowly defined scope. Using this type of partnership, two or more ongoing businesses can team up for a specific recording project and continue with their respective ongoing businesses without being wed together in other projects forever.

For example, a major production company possessing both a strong reputation and cash may decide to enter a joint venture agreement with a smaller, less experienced but artistically gifted company to produce one project together. While the smaller company may not be able to attract investment dollars to the project, the addition of the larger company's name lends the stability and experience that will entice money people to invest. If the project takes off, the joint venturers may decide to work on other projects together or start a separate and longer lasting business entity.

Corporations are very much like limited partnerships from the investor side, as the investor is relatively anonymous regarding the creative side of the artist's career. The amount of investment by "outsiders" dictates how much input they may have in the management of the company, which is usually admin-

istered through a board of directors voted on by the shareholders. Caution should be exercised if you're considering this vehicle, as it may require a great deal of time (and legal fees) to organize. Additionally, a number of formalities may be required by your state when it comes to incorporating. When choosing your form of business, it is best to consult with an experienced business advisor prior to raising money.

WHERE IS ALL THIS MONEY?

Unfortunately, there are no listings in your local telephone directory for "Benefactors." The money for financing a creative project usually comes from the Three Fs: family, friends, and fans. The Three Fs are more willing to front the money for your project if you have put some time and effort into your plan of attack, especially when it comes to explaining how they will be paid back. Be wary of investor types that prey on the talented yet broke by buying a piece of management, publishing, or artist royalties in exchange for what appears to be "an investment." (For a fictional case study, see the sidebar "Investors Gone Awry: A Cautionary Tale.") Additionally, I warn against seeking investors through want ads and the like without the assistance of counsel, as you may inadvertently violate federal and state securities regulations. (And you could get taken by a scam—big time.)

Any way you cut it,
you need to pay
back a loan.

FINALIZING THE DEAL

The more detailed your financial relationship (hopefully documented in writing with the aid of competent counsel), the fewer problems you may run into when royalties start to flow. Many start-up companies that formed as labors of love to support a handful of artists have blossomed into full-fledged businesses, subject to corporate buy-outs and mega-distribution deals. Of course, one of the most sophisticated and ideal investors is a legitimate record company that understands what you have and makes the investment of dollars, personnel, and reputation necessary to send your act into superstardom.

An investor wanting to get into the business may see your career as the entry point into the promised land of backstage passes and wild parties. Trading away a piece of your future to these investors might be enticing, but many investors involved in other business ventures do not realize how difficult it is to get a pay-off in the music industry. Remember that if you are carrying along extra baggage in the form of third-party investors looking for their share of the pie, your ticket to the show may be delayed until you straighten your affairs.

CHAPTER 20

Be Your Own Boss

The adage goes like this: If you want something done right, do it yourself. It is this DIY ethic that has spurred the current cottage industry of independent, self-produced CDs. And even though the home-studio boom has given musicians unprecedented control over the technical and creative aspects of their music, getting it out to the masses is as difficult as ever. Many musicians have decided to become their own bosses; so, in addition to producing their own music, they have taken over the music publishing, record label, and distribution chores for their releases.

The business aspects of starting a publishing company and/or a label are not much different from setting up any other type of business. You should select a name for your label and do a trademark search to make sure no one else has laid claim to the name; then, go ahead and file for your trademark. Your next step is to file a fictitious business-name statement, or a dba (doing business as), with your city or county clerk. Once that's done, you can obtain a resale license, a business license, and a federal tax identification number. These documents are all crucial in establishing your label as a legitimate business. You'll also need these licenses to open a bank account in your business's name.

All of this paperwork might seem like a hassle, but it makes good business sense. Setting up a separate legal entity for your business can protect your personal assets should your label enter dire financial straits. Also, be sure to carefully detail how the work and profits are to be divided if you are establishing the label or publishing company with bandmates or other individuals.

PUBLISHING BASICS

If you're not comfortable giving away or sharing the publishing rights to your songs (which you would do if you worked with a music publisher), you should consider establishing your own publishing company.

The first step in administering your own music publishing is to copyright the songs. The details of copyright are covered in chapter 25, "Comprehending Copyright," so we'll just do a quick review of the basics here. In short, copyright holders are entitled to five basic rights, including the right to issue mechanical licenses, perform the copyrighted works, make derivative works, display the works, and publish or exploit the works. The sources of income generated by the exploitation of copyrights of musical works are split into four main categories: print, synchronization, performance, and mechanical. The latter two—performance and mechanical—are the two most common you'll encounter as your own publisher.

Performance royalties generate a substantial amount of income for songwriters and publishers. By affiliating with ASCAP, BMI, or SESAC, the independent songwriter-publisher grants one of these performing rights societies the right to license use of the songs to radio, television, and so on; to collect

You should report all of your songs
to your performing-rights society so they will
show up on the survey of airplay.

the money generated from such use; and to pay out performance royalties. These organizations issue "blanket licenses" to users such as radio and television stations, allowing them to use all songs in each society's catalog. The license fees vary based on the size of the potential audience. A small restaurant with eight tables will pay a much smaller license fee than a 50,000 watt radio station with a large listening audience.

Songwriters and publishers inform their performing-rights societies of songs they have recorded and are likely to perform. Performing-rights societies then use a number of surveying techniques—including television logs of the songs and actual listening to radio stations—to determine approximately how often a song was performed and, in turn, what share of the total license revenue each song generated. A portion of this income is retained by the societies for administrative costs, and the balance is paid out to the songwriters and publishers of the various songs.

The easiest income to calculate for the independent writer-publisher is mechanical income. In order for a record label to manufacture and produce records containing a song, the copyright holder must issue a mechanical license to the label, setting forth the fee, the timing of payment (e.g., quarterly, semiannually), and any applicable restrictions regarding the sale of records using the song. Although the mechanical license fee is negotiable, the copyright tribunal (an administrative body established in accordance with the copyright law) sets a statutory rate for mechanical licenses. Currently, this rate is 6.95 cents/song per record sold. (That rate applies to songs that are five minutes in length or shorter; 1.1 cents is added to the rate for each minute or fraction thereof beyond five minutes.) Assuming sales of 100,000 units of a 10-song album (with all songs five minutes or shorter), $69,500 is generated from the use of the songs. This income is usually split evenly between the songwriters and publishers. If you are your own publisher, then you get to keep it all.

SELF-PUBLISHING

Most budding musicians are forced to self-publish simply because no one else is interested in doing it for them. But with so many artists making a go of it with independent releases, many are also opting to keep the publishing duties—and income—to themselves.

The primary roles of a publishing company are to *(a)* perform A&R duties; *(b)* be a salesperson of the writer's talents by finding writing and publishing opportunities, such as artists looking for songs, collaborations, or even shopping a record deal; and *(c)* handling the executive, administrative, and business duties, such as filing the copyright forms, cutting deals to share publishing expenses, interfacing with performing-rights societies, issuing mechanical licenses, and collecting the money.

If you find yourself able to perform most

If you're like most people
who start labels, you're long on ideas
and short on money.

of the duties listed above—particularly if you are releasing your own record—perhaps you should control your own copyrights. First of all, you'll need to follow the steps outlined above for establishing a business. Before filing for a fictitious business name statement in your county and investing in stationary and business cards, it would be wise to reserve your proposed publishing company name with the performing-rights society of your choice. Many writers are disappointed when they find out that the fanciful name they wanted to use for years is already in use by another publisher.

If your songs are being released by a third-party record company, you can either issue a mechanical license yourself with the aid of an entertainment lawyer or other music-savvy advisor or utilize the services of the Harry Fox Agency, a mechanical-licensing organization located in New York City that, for a small fee (usually about 4 to 5 percent of what they collect), issues mechanical licenses and collects and disperses the royalties to publishers. If you are putting out your own record, it is good practice to issue yourself a mechanical license to keep a clear business separation between your record-company activities and publishing activities.

Next, you should report all of your songs to your performing-rights society so they will show up on the survey of airplay. They cannot look for your songs if they are unaware of what they should be looking for, so don't overlook this detail.

Probably the most difficult task is finding homes for the songs. If you release your own record, you can generate income by expanding the uses of your songs by pitching them to bigger acts, independent multimedia and video producers, or independent-music supervisors looking for songs for films and/or TV. Let's face it, you will probably charge a lower sync fee than Sting, and you are also bringing them a master recording, so they can do one-stop shopping.

(For a complete guide to handling your own music publishing tasks, check out *Music Publishing: The Real Road to Success,* by Tim Whitsett, published by MixBooks)

A LABEL OF LOVE

As you're probably already painfully aware, major record labels offer little help to independent-minded and niche-market artists. In fact, many labels no longer sign acts unless *(a)* they've already sold scores of records, or *(b)* a small indie label has developed and marketed the artist to a certain sales and visibility level. As a result, many musicians are no longer waiting around to get signed by a label; they're creating their own.

It's not just a desire to sell their own music that has these artists starting labels. Some go into business with other musicians to pool resources and promote local artists. Other entrepreneurs have started labels because of a passion for certain hard-to-find styles of music. Whatever your reason for starting a record

You can bypass the distributor relationship by setting up your own mail-order company.

label, rest assured that it is more than just a difficult task; it is a labor of love.

KNOW WHAT YOU WANT

Before you spend your time and money setting up your label as a business, you need to have a good idea of what you're trying to accomplish. You don't have to go so far as to map out a ten-year blueprint to megamillion-dollar success, but you should have a good idea of why you want to create a label. Is it just an umbrella company under which you'll release only your own work? Perhaps you want to help other musicians in your area release their albums: they'll come to you with finished tracks, and you'll take care of distribution and promotion. Or maybe you want to actually sign and produce acts.

If you're like most people who start labels, you're long on ideas and short on money. And because you don't have the money to hire a staff, all of the legwork is up to you. You need to be the business manager, the promotions coordinator, the media contact, the new-talent scout, and maybe even the producer. These seemingly insurmountable tasks are reason enough not to go into business by yourself. By working with a partner or two, you can share the business expenses and the workload.

The best way to share the workload is according to talents. The two main roles you'll need to fill are those of schmoozer and accountant. The schmoozer should be the

person who loves to talk to other bands, follow up with distributors, and work with other important industry contacts. The money person must be a trustworthy and detail-oriented number-cruncher.

The most important skill you'll need, though, is a solid knowledge of how the industry works. This book is a good first step in learning how to work with industry execs, how to develop contacts, and how to plan various aspects of your career, but there is no substitute for going out there and just doing it.

GETTING IT OUT

The most labor-intensive aspect of running a label is making the public aware of your music. If you want your music sold in record stores, you need to line up distributors to carry your releases. Most artists with unproven track records will have serious difficulty persuading national or regional distributors to take on their releases. Don't just blindly mail out your CDs hoping to get a bite. Be sure to get a contact name at each distributor before you do your mailings. That way, you can send your release to the appropriate person, and you'll know who to call when it comes time to follow up. Distributors get hundreds of releases every week, so it's important to cultivate a relationship with people on the inside. Also, the music industry is built on hype, and every label lays claim to having "the next big thing." You need to prove that you or your artist has a decent enough following to make

Most budding musicians are forced to self-publish simply because no one else is interested in doing it for them.

the album worth a distributor's time and money.

If you can afford it, you might want to consider hiring the services of a music-promotion firm. These companies specialize in getting distribution deals for their clients. Also look into working with a small local distributor, if there are any in your area. Or, you can hoof it, meaning that you can go to all the local record stores and talk them into carrying your release on consignment.

Again, it all comes down to a sizable monetary investment. You have to front all the CDs to the record stores or distributors, then only after the stores or distributors have sold enough units to make their profits, you get your cut. It's a tough way to make a buck.

You can bypass the distributor relationship by setting up your own mail-order company or Internet retail distribution. The problem with that approach, though, is that it leaves you running *two* businesses, your label and the retail operation. But you don't have to run your own online presence: investigate participating in music newsgroups and music-related Web sites. Many newsgroups and sites specialize in promoting independent music. Also, the Web sites might provide another avenue for distributing your music without the hassles of maintaining your own site.

In addition to lining up distributors, you need to promote your artists to the record-buying public. So once again, the solution lies in hitting the phones and the pavement, building for yourself an extensive database of names and numbers. A good way to start that all important database is to rent a mailing list. These can be procured from magazines, mail-order catalogs, and retailers Furthermore, you'll need to gather information about radio stations that play your label's genre of music, media outlets for reviews, distributors, and maybe even contacts at larger labels, if you want any of your bands to get picked up.

You can also promote yourself by joining organizations that cater to independent musicians. One such organization is AFIM (Association for Independent Music). AFIM sponsors seminars for independent musicians and publishes a monthly catalog featuring members' releases. It goes out to much of the music industry, including distributors and the press, so it's a good way to generate interest in your music and keep your name circulating in the industry.

PARTING SHOTS

If running a publishing company and a label is this much work, why do people continue to do it? More often than not, it's a love of the music. If your sole desire is to get rich, then you're in for a tough time. But if you want to have as much control as possible over your music and your career, then you're doing it for the right reasons.

CHAPTER 21

The Taxman

One of the most overlooked aspects in a musician's career is the tax ramifications of doing business. In a world of overnight successes, where bands go from handing out cassettes at small bars to supporting platinum-selling CDs with arena tours, the dramatic swings in income can be a kiss of death for the artist who didn't bother to plan for the Taxman. For most of us, fear of a tax audit ranks right up there with a root canal *sans* anesthesia. A musician's taxes tend to be complicated because most artists don't exactly punch a clock. As such, an artist's journey through the tax maze is fraught with potential stumbling blocks.

A TAXING SITUATION

Let's start with the basics. The federal government is empowered to tax the income of its citizens, which it does via the Internal Revenue Service. Additionally, each state may tax its residents based on income and for doing business in the state (e.g., sales taxes and property taxes). Counties and cities may also tax those who are residing and/or doing business within their jurisdiction. It is your responsibility to determine which local tax laws apply to you. State and local tax codes vary so much that I will limit our discussion to the major considerations regarding federal taxes.

Your income from *all sources* is taxable income. Time and time again, we read about prominent figures who neglected to report some of their income and ended up having to pay the piper in a big way. Income you receive from gigs, session work, synthesizer and drum-machine programming, royalties, and any other music-related work is taxable income. One way the federal government makes sure that you are not receiving certain income "under the table" is to require the entities paying you (e.g., record companies, night clubs, producers) to report to both you and the IRS how much money they paid to you during the year.

THE RIGHT TO WRITE OFF

A common fallacy in the music business is that every nickel an artist spends is a tax deduction (also called a *write-off*). It is easy to fall into the mental trap of thinking that the more money you lose, the better off you are, because such losses offset the money that you make at your day job. This is not true. If you lose money at your business too many years in a row, the IRS doesn't consider it a business anymore; it is merely a hobby. The costs involved in pursuing a hobby are not deductible, no matter how promising your band's prospects.

Let's say you've determined that your music career is a business. Now you're ready to benefit from the same write-offs other business people have enjoyed for years. What are these write-offs? The general rule is that you can take deductions for *ordinary and necessary expenses* in connection with running your busi-

If you lose money at your business too many years in a row, the IRS doesn't consider it a business anymore; it is merely a hobby.

ness. If a deduction looks out of the ordinary or unnecessary, it may come under IRS scrutiny and trigger an audit. Following are some of the common, allowable expenses that most musicians encounter.

Studio/rehearsal/office-space rental. Whether you rent on an hourly, daily, or monthly basis, this expense is commonly considered to be reasonable. The IRS is sometimes inspired to take a closer look at write-offs that involve a "home office/studio" space. Many write-offs for home space are denied because the space was not used *solely and exclusively* for the business. When planning your home studio, make sure that it will be used only for your business purposes and will not double as a living area. The size of the deduction is usually based on the percentage of the entire space taken up by the work area (e.g., your studio takes 15 percent of your house, so your deduction is equivalent to 15 percent of your rent/house payment).

Equipment purchase/lease. Musicians, studio owners, producers, and gear-hungry artists go crazy over this potential write-off. There is good news and bad news when it comes to equipment purchases. Yes, you can write off equipment purchases. However, there is a dollar limit on how much you may write off. So before you run out and buy a fully automated $500,000 mixing console, be sure to speak to your tax advisor about what the limits are. Many musicians are opting to lease equipment because—based on the deal they make with a leasing company—they have

the flexibility of updating their equipment while writing off the lease payments, thus avoiding the dollar-limit imposed on purchases.

Recording costs/fees. If you rent a recording studio for your projects, the costs related to the recording are potential deductions. This includes studio rental, mastering fees, engineer costs, and related expenses.

Professional services. Fees that you pay to lawyers, accountants, studio-design consultants, and session players are all potential write-offs. Because these professionals are working for you, you should provide them with an IRS 1099 miscellaneous-income form at the end of the year. If over the course of the year you pay more than $600 to any of your independent contractors, you are required to submit a copy of their 1099 form to the IRS, as well.

Travel and entertainment. Take one look at the headlines about politicians under fire from the IRS, and you can figure out that the ordinary and necessary limits of travel expenses are being tested on a daily basis. Hotel and truck-rental costs incurred by your band for touring are probably allowable. Your bender with a bunch of "cool dudes" you met in Fargo, North Dakota, is probably not allowable, unless you can prove that it was in furtherance of your business purpose (perhaps one of the "cool dudes" was a booking agent). A trip to the Bahamas to "get your head together" is questionable, whereas a trip to Cannes, France, for a music conference is

The key to all financial management in your career is impeccable record keeping.

probably allowable.

Only a small percentage of your business meals may be written off, so don't be so anxious to pick up that check at your local restaurant just for the sake of getting the write-off. Plan accordingly and determine the purpose of your actions before you assume it is an automatic write-off.

Supplies. Many musicians confuse supplies with equipment. Many musicians also neglect to write off their supplies. The money spent on pens, pencils, stationery, audio- and videotape, computer supplies, and the like adds up to a substantial amount when the day is done.

Education and conferences. From taking a MIDI course at your local junior college to attending a major recording-industry seminar, anything done to further your skill and knowledge in connection with your career is a potential write-off. Along this same line, books and trade-magazine subscriptions are also are allowable.

Postage, phone, and related costs. Don't overlook deductions for costs associated with promotional efforts. Photocopying, faxing charges, overnight-mail delivery fees, and telephone bills add up to a substantial amount of money and are possible write-offs for your business.

There's more. The list of potential deductions goes on, depending on how creative you and your tax advisor wish to be (within the limits of what is ordinary and necessary, of course). These other deductions include union dues, voice lessons, photo costs, automobile expenses, equipment-insurance costs, and so on.

WILL I HAVE TO DO TIME?

As you're probably aware, the IRS conducts audits, sometimes randomly and sometimes based on specific questions raised by a tax return. Don't hit the panic button and begin planning your escape from a federal penitentiary yet. An audit is simply a meeting with an IRS agent to determine whether you have indeed paid the correct amount of tax. If you are prepared and have a well-documented case, keeping all receipts and being able to justify all of your expenses, you will survive an audit.

If your case is complicated, you may wish to enlist the aid of a professional, such as an accountant or tax lawyer, to advise you or even attend the audit. Be prepared to spend some money for these professional services, though, as they are sometimes time consuming and such consultants bill on an hourly basis. If some of your expenses are disallowed, you may be liable for the unpaid taxes and penalties based on the adjusted income from the audit.

CYA WITH A CPA

With the decentralization of the federal government, states and municipalities are taxing more aggressively than ever. For traveling musicians especially, particular attention

*If some of your expenses are disallowed,
you may be liable for the unpaid
taxes and penalties.*

must be given to those states that have gone after—and collected taxes from—visiting sports figures earning money in their states. If you do a 20-city tour spanning four states, be prepared to deal with four different state tax codes for the money earned in each state.

The key to all financial management in your career is impeccable record keeping. A number of financial-management software programs are available that can help you keep good records. Federal tax laws are changing daily, so be sure to enlist the aid of a competent tax advisor to assist you. Personal referrals from people you know and legal-referral services should be of help. It is important to choose a tax professional you are comfortable with and who is familiar with the entertainment industry.

CHAPTER 22

From Song to Screen

Original music is an integral part of most movies and television shows, be it in the form of themes for opening or closing credits, short segues between scenes, or long background pieces. Film and TV production companies hire musicians for a variety of services, ranging from music composition to actually recording and producing the music.

Let's first look at how music finds its way into film and television, then we'll look at how *your* music can find its way there.

When it comes to composing film and television music, the scorer works closely with the director, producer, and other decision makers to develop a distinctive sound that supports the film's or show's style and visual images. A few rounds of rewriting are not uncommon for the scorer. First of all, edits and revisions in story lines are commonplace; and secondly, it can take a few tries for the scorer to nail just what the producer and director are looking for. (For the lowdown on music for advertisements, see chapter 23, "Going Commercial.")

The advent of reasonably priced professional recording equipment has made it possible for composers to provide directors and producers with a finished product. The scorer/music producer benefits from this all-in deal by having more creative control over the sound of the work and by increasing the fees charged by providing the entire service. The producer and director benefit by doing "one-stop shopping," which lets them deal with only one creative mind and business entity. On the down side, some composers and music producers have grumbled that all-in deals have increased competition by shrinking the opportunities for composers and producers.

WANNA BUY A USED SONG?

Music for television and movies often comes from *catalog music,* which consists of compositions previously owned by a music publisher and not written specifically for the project at hand. Many times, these are songs originally released as phonograph records. From the Isley Brothers telling us "It's Your Thing" on Burger King commercials to the launching of an unknown rock band via a movie soundtrack, an increasing number of publishing companies are exploiting their music catalogs on the big and small screens.

Most major music-publishing companies have divisions devoted to placing songs in movies and television. The publishing representative works constantly on developing and maintaining movie industry contacts, reads industry trade magazines, visits production companies, and sends out promotional CDs and demos to production companies looking for music. If you're interested in having your music promoted to film companies, you should work with a publisher that is experienced in that area of the business. It's also to your advantage to make sure your publisher knows you and your work well.

The first thing to do when making a cold call is to get the name of the person responsible for hiring music.

A good match between a song and a scene in a movie, television show, or commercial can substantially increase the visual image's impact on the viewer. For these reasons, the picking and choosing of songs for a project is left to a very important person called the *music supervisor*. The music supervisor works closely with the producers of the show, *spotting* the movie or television episode for the scenes requiring music and taking note of what style of music is necessary, how long each use should be, and how much of the production budget is set aside to acquire music rights. The music supervisor then goes to all of his or her music contacts (primarily music publishers), finds the right pieces for the production, and proceeds to negotiate the fees for the uses.

And it's not just megastars that get songs placed in movies. Sometimes a scene will call for a song playing quietly on a radio in the background. If the song is too well known, it will detract from the scene. Music supervisors will work with a publisher to choose an appropriate song from a specific genre to fill the bill.

The music supervisor's job is not simply an administrative or legal position. This job requires a great deal of creativity and intuition. It also requires working closely with the producer and director to develop (and argue over) the best music for the show.

FOLLOW THE MONEY TRAIL

Let's look now at the sources of income generated by movie and television scores. A scorer receives a *composing fee* for composing the music for a particular project. If the scorer can deliver the goods, the payoff can be substantial. Fees for television background scores can range from a "breaking in for the experience" low of only a few hundred dollars for a half-hour TV episode to the several thousand dollars per episode that an experienced composer can charge. These figures change dramatically for film scoring: the top film scorers can command scoring fees well into the hundreds of thousands of dollars for a major motion picture.

Synchronization fees are fees paid by the film or television producer in connection with a synchronization license—a license issued by the copyright holder of a song to allow the song to be reproduced on film or for television in synchronization with the visual images. The fee for a sync license varies based on a number of factors, including how popular the song was, whether the song will be revised to fit a particular use (e.g., substituting a product name into the lyrics of a song), how much of the song is used in the final version of the visual work, and how large of a budget is available to the music supervisor to spend on music. While an independent film maker or television production house may only wish to spend a few hundred dollars for a sync license, it is not out of the ordinary

*It's not just
megastars that get songs
placed in movies.*

for an advertising agency to spend several hundred thousand dollars to use a song for a major advertising campaign, nor is it unusual for a major motion picture production company to spend tens of thousands of dollars for the right song for the right scene. When you're negotiating sync licenses, an experienced music publisher or attorney can advise you on the fair valuation of your work and give you a realistic view of your bargaining position.

Performance royalties are generated from broadcast uses of a piece of music. The user is required to keep a cue sheet of all of the music used in connection with the visual work. Your performing rights society then collects and distributes the royalties generated from the broadcast of the music. Note that performance royalties are above and beyond the synchronization fees paid to use the music, so you can reap the rewards from both sources.

The *master license* and *production fee* are also potential sources of income if you are delivering a finished work rather than simply handing over a song that needs to be rerecorded by another producer. The composer who self-produces has a head start if the film or television producer is looking for finished material.

I WANT IN ON THIS

Sounds good so far, but how do you get in on this? Unfortunately, it's not easy. Like most suc-

cess in the entertainment industry, getting your music placed in film and TV depends on who you know and who's stumping for you, but most importantly, it depends on your ability.

For one thing, you must be able to write music on demand, not just when the inspiration hits you. You also need to be able to write music that sets the appropriate mood for the project you're working on, which means you must be well versed in a variety of musical styles. You'll also need the ability to score to picture. The more comfortable you are working with picture, the less you'll have to think about the mechanics of it and the more you'll be able to concentrate on the musical aspects. Finally, you must be able to handle the fast turnaround times and heavy deadline pressures that are endemic to the business.

As a commercial composer, you won't have control over your own work, instead you'll need to take direction from and communicate regularly with those who hire you. What's more, you'll be expected to produce the demos—and often the final versions—in your own studio using your own equipment. This means you need to function as a composer, arranger, and producer as well as an engineer. If you want to compete for this kind of work, you must be able to produce high-quality, professional-sounding tracks.

If you're interested in pursuing film and television work, your best bet is to start off small. Without any credits to your name, you probably won't get considered for many high-profile gigs, but that doesn't mean you can't

*You must be able to handle the fast
turnaround times and heavy deadline pressures
that are endemic to the business.*

get steady work while working to make a name for yourself.

If you're a songwriter, push your publisher to shop your existing work to music supervisors. For film scoring experience, investigate opportunities to work on small, local, independent films. For example, local art schools or other colleges might be a good source for movies and multimedia projects that need music. Sure, these jobs might not pay much, if anything, but think of it as an investment in your career. Lastly, research the possibility of doing advertising scores for local radio and television ads or scores for locally produced television shows. All these bits and pieces of work will help you hone your chops and contribute to your reel, which you'll need if you want to continue to shop your work to producers and music supervisors.

PUTTING TOGETHER A REEL

No matter what kind of commercial composing work you're pursuing, you'll need a demo tape—known in industry jargon as a *reel*—in order to show your stuff. Generally speaking, you can get by with an audio reel when you're first starting out, but a video version is preferable because it demonstrates your ability to score to picture.

Depending on what type of work you're going after, you'll need to tailor your reel accordingly. If you're pursuing jobs in multiple areas, you'll ideally have a number of reels specifically tailored to the different types of

work. Here are some general guidelines that apply to just about all reels.

Keep it short and sweet. You can be sure that the people who are listening to or watching your reel are inundated with tapes and videos from composers and will only pay attention to yours if it grabs them right away—so put your best stuff first! With audio reels especially, it's effective to use relatively short segments of your various pieces (figure 30 seconds as the maximum length) that are edited tightly together with crossfades in between.

Fake the experience. If you don't have any commercial work to put on your reel, you can use examples of your songwriting (in an edited form), or you can write and produce material specifically for the reel. Some people even tape movie or television scenes, write music for them, and use them on their video reels. Although it's preferable to show actual jobs that you've done, the most important thing is to be able to demonstrate your ability to write and produce good quality music.

Format considerations. Audio reels can be on cassette, but CDs sound better and make you look more happening. As for video reels, some production companies and ad agencies will request that you send them in 3/4-inch (U-Matic) format, but these are quite costly to duplicate, and you can get by with VHS copies most of the time. Whatever type of reel you're sending out, make sure that you put printed, professional-looking labels on them with your name and contact information prominently displayed.

Depending on what type of work you're going after, you'll need to tailor your reel accordingly.

SHOPPING YOUR REEL

To land composing work, you'll have to pursue it aggressively, marketing yourself to producers, agencies, and clients by calling around and sending out your reel. It can be a very time-consuming and frustrating process.

The first thing to do when making a cold call is to get the name of (and hopefully talk to) the person responsible for hiring music and find out if he or she is at all interested in checking out your reel. Making an appointment to meet in person is the best way to go, but most people will instead ask you to send them a reel. When you do, include a cover letter mentioning your strengths and your previous credits.

After allowing a couple of weeks to give them a chance to listen, follow up with a phone call. Be prepared for a lot of rejection; people generally prefer to hire those they know and trust rather than take a chance on an unknown quantity. Nevertheless, if you can impress them with your talent and a strong, well-packaged reel, you're likely to generate interest from some producers or other potential clients.

In the highly competitive world of commercial composing, you can initially increase your odds of succeeding by aiming at the lower-profile areas of the field. Once you get your foot in the door, you can then begin to build your contacts and your reel so that eventually you can go after the more glamorous work.

CHAPTER 23

Going Commercial

Want to follow in the song-writing footsteps of Barry Manilow? Start by penning the lyrics to a soft-drink commercial. Trying to crack the Top 40 *and* put food on the table? Sing television and radio jingles. It worked for Luther Vandross. Or maybe you're looking for a way to pay for all that recording equipment in your living room.

Many musicians deride scoring for advertisements as the ultimate sell out. Sell is the operative word, though not necessarily an expletive. Just because you write a 30-second song praising the benefits of Brand X dog food, doesn't mean you can't write an opera, too. The dog food spot can cover your bills while your true musical passion pours elsewhere.

The best part of the job is the flexibility. The increased affordability of high-tech tools makes it possible to record ready-for-broadcast productions in the comfort of your home studio. And because commercial gigs usually have short turn-around times, you can squeeze them in between other jobs. In addition to flexibility, commercial scoring has another advantage over other areas of the music business: It pays, and sometimes it pays quite well.

HAWKING YOUR GOODS

Let's say you've decided to pursue scoring for commercials. Before you even consider approaching a prospective client about work, do your homework. Scrutinize television and radio ads. Don't just look for what you like or don't like; listen for prevalent styles and attention-getting scores. Also, take note of musical structures: how long the average intro is, when the music fades for voice-overs, and so on.

Once you think you have a feel for what works and what doesn't, try your hand at writing a few sample commercials. You'll need these samples to put together a demo or a reel. That's right, a demo. This is just like shopping for a record deal, unpleasant legwork and all. (See chapter 22, "From Song to Screen," for tips on putting together and shopping your reel.)

Now it's time to hit the streets. Send your reel to local ad execs, businesses, and jingle production houses. All the usual rules of self-promotion apply: include a concise, typewritten cover letter, contact numbers, and any pertinent musical credits. Don't forget follow-up letters and phone calls, but remember that harassing people seldom works. If you do encounter rejection, ask for a critique of your work so you can fine tune it for further submissions. Also, if finding work directly from ad agencies or businesses proves a dead end, a production house might be willing to bring you in to help out on an as-needed basis.

But let's face it, starting out cold is the pits. The best way to drum up business is through contacts in your local music community. You still need the reel and the polite but firm self-promotional skills, but any connection is better than none. In fact, it's well known that word of mouth is the best way to get work.

*Always get the contract and money
matters settled up front, before you record
a single note.*

WHAT TO EXPECT

Getting clients is only the tip of the iceberg; you still have to deliver the goods. Your first reality check is that your people skills are as important as you musical chops. And remember that the ad execs you'll be dealing with are under a great deal of stress. Their careers depend on how well their ad spots are drumming up business and name recognition for their clients.

The first application of your all-important people skills is asking the right questions of your client. Again, if you've done your homework, you'll have a point of reference when your client starts naming commercials he or she likes. More often than not, a client is not musically articulate, so it's up to you to help them get the sound they want.

One approach is what's called a "needle drop" session with your client, in which you play small bits of twenty or so spots to see which ones are close to what the client wants. From there, you can question the client about exactly what he or she liked in those needle-drop spots. This trial-and-error method is not unusual.

The composer can be brought into the ad-creation process at any point. Of course, most composers prefer to be consulted at the outset, but that's not usually the case. If the ad is based around the song, your work will come first; but more often than not, the music is the very last thing, and they'll usually come to you just barely before or past their deadline.

In short, be ready for anything. The turn-around time for commercials is amazingly short. In the span of two to three days, you'll meet with your client, do a quick demo to make sure you're on the right track, send it back to the client for feedback, make your changes, record the final piece, send it back to the client, make the final tweaks, master it, watch it synched to the visuals with voice-overs, make any tweaks necessitated by those elements, and ship it off. Entertain no delusions of this as a quick 'n' easy way to make money; it's an incredibly difficult job.

HIRED GUN

As with all things you do as a musician and composer, you need to consider the financial aspect. And with commercial work (including film and television scoring) there are a few added complexities.

Most commercial work is done on a "work for hire" basis, which means that the person who hired you owns the rights to the music after you have created it. Until you have some clout in the business, you can expect to work this way frequently. This type of agreement is also referred to as a "buy-out," which means that you are getting all of the payments owed to you—up front—that you expect to receive for this project. This is not necessarily a bad thing: in certain situations you may end up getting paid more than you would waiting for residuals or performance royalties. It all depends on the frequency and territory of broadcast.

More often than not, a client is not musically articulate, so it's up to you to help them get the sound they want.

If you are trying to get work with ad agencies, you would benefit from being in the Musician's Union because many agencies have union contracts. If the project is broadcast nationally, is not a buy-out, and is a union gig, you can expect residuals that can add up to some serious money.

There are also hybrid payment schemes that allow for varying degrees of financial remuneration. For example, you might be offered a work-for-hire project in which the composition rights are licensed back to the composer. That means, in addition to getting paid for creating the music, the production company would give you back the composition rights but keep the publishing rights—a substantial sum if it's a successful ad campaign and a memorable tune. Another common practice is to be asked to do the job for no up-front payment in return for keeping the composition rights. The rationale for this offer is that the performance royalties will be payment enough for the composer. If you're just starting out and are hungry for the business, this is good a way to get your feet wet and develop your reel.

IT'S A WRAP

Even though your job as composer is difficult, part of that job is putting your client at ease. You have to be able to communicate well with them. If they know they can talk to you, then they will come back and will recommend you to others, especially if you can make them look good.

Here are some last bits of advice: Always get the contract and money matters settled up front, before you record a single note. This little piece of common sense applies to any business dealing, musical or otherwise. Once everyone knows where they stand, the creative process moves much more smoothly. Also, you have to keep promoting yourself. The biggest names in the business have reels, CDs, and brochures detailing their most recent work, along with publicists to send them out and follow up.

The final and most important piece of advice is that you must be an excellent, versatile musician who can conjure up creativity on the spot. Without those skills, you don't stand much of a chance in this competitive area of the entertainment industry.

SECTION

4

The Fine Print

Important Legal Details
Every Musician Should Know

CHAPTER 24

Legal Checklist for Releasing Your Album

L et's say you have produced your own album and will hit the market with it. You've probably given careful consideration to the technical and creative aspects of your album, but have you accorded the same scrutiny to the legal agreements related to the production and release of the record?

Chances are that you worked with some other musicians while making your album. But even if you recorded and produced the entire album yourself, you may have enlisted the aid of a graphic artist to design the CD cover or borrowed money to get the project off the ground. These contributors could lay legal claim to some of your album's profits. And don't forget that any samples incorporated into your production may put you at risk for copyright infringement. Securing all the proper legal agreements up front can save you from any nasty surprises in civil court.

ESTABLISHING YOUR RIGHTS

The initial step in the legal process is filing an SR (Sound Recording) Copyright Registration form with the Register of Copyrights. This document establishes your ownership rights to the master recording, signifies your exclusive right to make copies and derivative works, allows you to play the record in public, and lets you deal these rights to others.

Remember that the rights to the master recording are separate and distinct from any rights to the *compositions* used on the master.

So if you also wrote all the songs, be sure to register those as well with copyright form PA, which covers published or unpublished works of the performing arts.

PERSONNEL ISSUES

If you hire any artist to work on your album, a written agreement is a no-brainer. The following types of legal arrangements should be considered before you start recording.

Musician release forms. These are releases that session musicians, background vocalists, and additional production personnel sign acknowledging that they have been paid for their services. The release also states that the individual has no ownership claim to the recording and that he or she allows you to use his or her name and likeness in connection with selling the record. Many records have been held up from release because hired contributors felt that their compensation was unfair or that they deserved royalty payments instead of a one-time fee for their services. Be forewarned that if your record is picked up by a major record label, the services of musicians or vocalists may come under the jurisdiction of the American Federation of Musicians' or the American Federation of Television and Recording Artists' collective bargaining agreements—regardless of the set fee you paid.

Independent-producer contracts. In today's music market, the career of a producer can be launched by the success of one act. Likewise, the success of an act can be launched by its

When hiring an outside promoter, be very clear about the terms of your agreement.

alliance with a "hot" producer. Because of this, producer agreements are no longer the same as the musician contracts mentioned above. These agreements have evolved to full-blown negotiations over producer advances, royalties (also known as *points*) from sales of records, as well as what type, size, and frequency of credits the producer will receive in connection with the project.

Graphic artist/design agreements. This is a legal area that seems straightforward, but there are several aspects of the agreement you might not have thought about. Are you paying a flat fee for the design and production of the cover artwork for your project? Who eventually will own the artwork? Is the graphic artist doing the work as a "work for hire"? Can you use the artwork for posters, T-shirts, and other promotional materials? Can you alter the artwork? Be sure to address all of these issues at the outset of your collaboration with an artist or designer.

SONGWRITING AND PUBLISHING

If any of the material on your release was written by a third party, whether or not they have previously recorded it, you are well advised to stick to the law regarding issues of copyright, mechanical licenses, and sample clearances.

Mechanical licenses. According to the copyright law, anyone wishing to include a musical composition on a medium that requires a mechanical device to play the song, such as a CD or a cassette, must obtain a *mechanical license* from the copyright holder. This license includes details such as the express permission of the copyright holder to the manufacturer and distributor to include the song on a release, the amount of royalty to be paid, and when it is to be paid. Accordingly, it is imperative that this license be obtained by you prior to release, especially if yours is the first recording of the song.

If you are covering previously released material, you can track down the copyright holder by checking out the publisher credit on the original album. You can also contact the research department of one of the major performing-rights societies and request the current publisher of a song. This type of information can be accessed at the ASCAP, BMI, and SESAC Web sites (www.ascap.com, www.bmi.com, and www.sesac.com, respectively).

However, if the songs on your album are self-published, keep in mind that your rights as a publisher are separate from your rights as an artist and record company. It's good practice to issue a mechanical license from your publishing company to your record company. That way, if you license or sell off the rights to your record, your publishing and administration rights to the compositions will be clearly defined.

Sample clearances. The letter of the law is simple: Thou shalt not sample and make derivative works of others' copyrighted works without their express permission. Trade publications and legal journals are full of copyright-infringement cases involving multiplatinum-selling

Thou shalt not sample and make derivative works of others' copyrighted works without their express permission.

artists who have to pay out big dollars because they didn't bother to clear samples. Remember that clearing a sample requires the permission of two separate copyright holders: the owner of the copyright to the composition (a publishing company) and the owner of the copyright of the master (a record company). Obtain the services of an entertainment attorney or a sample-clearing service if you're not confident tackling this task yourself.

When negotiating a sample clearance, you need to consider the following points: the territory of your authorized use of the sample (e.g., U.S. only or worldwide); the price you are paying for the sample; whether or not there will be an ongoing royalty paid to the party issuing the sample clearance; who owns the new work (be it a master or composition); what credits are to be given to the original copyright holder; and whether you have to obtain the original copyright holder's permission for other uses (e.g., using the sample in a video or remix).

Collaboration and publishing agreements. Deciding how to split writing and publishing royalties can become the biggest legal debate you encounter when releasing an independent record. A project can come to a standstill over the issue of whether the principals can agree to a 50/50 songwriting split instead of a 60/40 split.

In addition, many independent labels seek to participate in the publishing rights to songs. These valuable rights require publishing agreements that spell out what the pub-

lishing splits will be, who is entitled to administer those rights, and what should happen to those rights if the act subsequently takes off on a major label. Music history shows that the premature selling of publishing rights to independent companies in the early stages of a writer's career can result in a multimillion dollar return for major corporations later. In short, don't be pressured into signing a bad deal that may haunt you forever. The publishing rights that Little Richard sold off in the 1950s, for example, are still generating income for their current owner, Michael Jackson.

MONEY, MONEY, MONEY

Everything we've discussed so far has dealt with money: who gets how much and when. Now we need to deal with the procurement and disbursement of the green stuff itself. Investors and creditors may not contribute artistically to your project, but they do make it financially possible for you to record and release your album. And, more often than not, these folks aren't just doing this out of the goodness of their hearts. They want their cut, too.

Studio "spec" agreements. One of the most misunderstood and abused principles in the recording industry is the spec (short for *speculative*) agreement. Basically, these agreements allow an artist to use a recording studio and its personnel for cheap—or even for nothing—in exchange for payment later, when "something happens." It is wise to nego-

*Don't be pressured into
signing a bad deal that may
haunt you forever.*

tiate and agree upon specific occurrences and dollar figures, including the number of hours being allotted to the project, what the premium studio rate is going to be, and exactly what events trigger the eventual payment (e.g., a major label picks up the project for distribution).

Investment and/or loan agreements. When dealing with financial supporters—especially family and friends—be sure to secure agreements that set forth the terms and conditions of the loan or investment. These agreements should include how the money will be used, what the repayment scenario will be, and what the risk is for the creditors/investors. Working out these issues in advance is the best way to ensure a civil relationship if your record doesn't go multiplatinum as you promised it would.

If someone loans you money for your project, look at reasonable commercial loan rates to determine a reasonable repayment rate, the sources you will be using to repay the money, and when you will be expected to pay back the loan. This way, the deal is more business-like and straightforward—a much less stressful scenario than dealing with excessively high loan-shark rates or relationship-testing "friend and family" rates.

OTHER AGREEMENTS AND LEGALITIES

Okay, you have your session-musician agreements settled, you've cleared all the samples that appear on your album, and you've worked out your investor-repayment scenario. You're all set to release your record, right? Not so fast. You also need to consider the people who make it possible to get your music out to the masses.

Promotion agreements. In general, promoters work to generate sales for your record via retail, radio, and "street" promotions, such as fan clubs and other grassroots-type go-out-and-get-your-audience schemes. They often do give-aways at concerts, clubs, schools, and anywhere else they can generate a "buzz."

When hiring an outside promoter, be very clear about the terms of your agreement. Important points of your agreement should include how long the promoter will work your record, what geographical region his or her efforts will encompass, what kind of reports you will be provided to help you track the album's progress, how closely he or she will work with your touring and self-promotion scheduling, and what the fee will be for all of this work.

Agent agreements. An independent record is often released as part of a larger plan to get the attention of a major record label and secure a deal. Part of this process is hiring an agent to shop the deal for you. Decide the limits of the agent's authority, what his or her fee will be, and whether he or she will remain involved in your career after a major-label deal is made.

Lawyer-engagement agreements. With all of these contracts to be negotiated, you might want to consider hiring a lawyer. Lawyers can

One of the most misunderstood and abused principles in the recording industry is the spec agreement.

also take on the role of shopping deals, as described above. Fee arrangements range from hourly fees to working for a percentage of your record deal. Again, attention should be given to detailing the lawyer's duties and what any royalty percentages will be based on.

Band agreements. A difficult task is determining how the members of the act will be compensated when the record (hopefully) takes off. For example, are all the members of a group going to participate equally in the "record company" share of the release? Perhaps only one or two members take on the administrative and business responsibilities of getting the record out and expect to be compensated accordingly. And what if one of the band members owns the studio where the album was recorded? What happens with the royalties or the record company if the group breaks up? All of these details should be worked out by the group in band-partnership agreements.

Trademark issues. As you are probably distributing your record under a label name, it is important that releasing the record will not infringe upon any other company's trademark. If you receive a cease-and-desist letter from a company across the country and your record is only intended for a limited geographical release, perhaps you should consider negotiating a "use" license of the name for your specific purpose and geographical area.

License and tax issues. Depending on your local and state laws, you may be required to obtain a reseller's license in order to sell your product. Additionally, you may be required to charge and pay taxes for doing business as a record company. Any and all monies made from the sales of records are subject to federal, state, and local taxation, so be sure to keep your books accurate and stay on top of the appropriate laws. You should also familiarize yourself with the tax laws concerning the hiring of independent contractors (e.g., session musicians). You may be required to file federal tax forms, as the independent contractor is responsible for paying taxes on his or her income.

LAST LOOK

Daunting as it may seem, releasing an independent record shouldn't be a drag. In general, simple written agreements that cover the major points discussed here should do the trick. If you are concerned about the amount of paperwork involved, retain the services of an experienced entertainment lawyer or other advisor to handle the documentation of your various deals.

CHAPTER 25

Comprehending Copyright

Today's musicians are surrounded by copyright issues, from the ownership of software to the ownership of lyrics. This chapter certainly isn't a definitive reference, but it should underscore this law's importance to your career.

Originally enacted in 1909, the United States Copyright Law is found in Title 17 of the United States Code, a dry piece of work with a supporting body of extraordinary case law. The cast of copyright-infringement actions range from major record labels to *Mad* magazine to famous artists in every field of expression.

WHAT IS COPYRIGHTABLE?

A copyrightable work is the *expression* of ideas, not the idea itself. For instance, developing an idea for a rock song about a woman named Susie entitled "Eighteen-Wheeler Heart-Stealer From Kentucky" does not entitle you to file copyright infringement actions against every composer who lamented a woman named Susie, invoked the state of Kentucky, or referenced big trucks in their songs. However, once the idea is communicated via a tangible form (a demo tape, lyric sheet, or sequencer file), the work is copyrightable. Titles of songs are generally not copyrightable, as they rarely express a complete idea.

There also is confusion over the distinction between the copyright of musical works and the right to copyright master recordings, which was included in the copyright law as a protection against counterfeiting. Musicians need to understand that the right to own a composition (song) is distinct from the right to own a recording, i.e., a master tape or phonorecord. Phonorecord is defined as "the physical object which embodies the work of authorship," such as compact discs, tapes, or records. Let's say you decide to produce a CD of your own compositions along with a cover version of "Pump It Up" by Elvis Costello. Upon completion of the project, you would own the rights to your master tape and the rights to your compositions. However, simply recording "Pump It Up" does not give you the rights to the Elvis Costello song, just the rights to your *master recording* of his composition. You must pay the mechanical license fee to the copyright holder if you want to include his or her composition on your CD.

CREATIVE DIVISION

When it comes to songwriting and copyright, collaboration can be a scary subject. Countless disputes have arisen over song ownership when groups compose by jamming together or when writers shuffle parts. ("I've got a great rhythm track; can you write a melody and lyrics over it?") Collaborators often forget the importance of converting creative contributions to a finished work into percentages of ownership. It's difficult to decide—especially *after* a song sells 1 million records—whether to attribute the work's popularity to its cool bass line, lyrics, vocal melody, or synthesizer licks.

Collaborators often forget the importance of converting creative contributions to a finished work into percentages of ownership.

Creative isolation prevents song-ownership conflicts, but it is hardly fun (or practical) for most composers to write in exile. It's better to forge a written agreement with collaborators, particularly if royalty income is to be unevenly distributed. This agreement should include a detailed description of each writer's contribution, the percentage of ownership earned by that contribution, whether one writer has the authority to speak for the other, and what happens if the original work is altered, or whether it even *can* be altered. (See chapter 1, "Collaboration Without Combat," for advice on musical collaborations.)

Of note here is the concept of a "work for hire" agreement. If a composer is commissioned by a third party to create a work, the registered owner and "author" of the copyright is the third party who commissioned the work. Be sure to immediately establish whether your commission is a work for hire. If it is, you won't own any of the compositions you are contracted to write.

FORMALITIES

Registering your composition with the Library of Congress gives it a recognized proof of ownership and avails the copyright holder a number of legal remedies should his or her rights be compromised. Registration of a work requires filling out form PA, available from the Register of Copyrights (tel. 202/707-9100; Web lcweb.loc.gov/copyright/reg.html), and filing it with a copy of the score or record-ing. Your nearest federal government printing office or a local entertainment lawyer also may dispense these forms. The current registration fee is $20.

Some musicians wonder if they can save registration fees by mailing a tape to themselves in a sealed envelope, or by registering all their songs under one song title. While these methods are acceptable, some qualifications and cautions exist. If you do not register your work with the Library of Congress, certain remedies, including statutory money damages, are unavailable should someone infringe on your copyright. Also, registering a number of songs under one title may cause the transfer of rights to all songs registered on the same form, when a third party may intend to buy only a single work. The general rule is that the investment in correctly registering your songs is minute compared to the costs of protecting unregistered work should a dispute arise.

THE COPY "RIGHTS"

The copyright holder of a musical work is entitled to five exclusive sets of rights: the right to issue mechanical licenses to produce records or print sheet music; the right to perform the copyrighted work; the right to make derivative works; the right to display (traditionally related to visual works but is now becoming important for use of musical works in multimedia "displays" of music via the Internet or visual presentations); and finally,

The investment in correctly registering your songs is minute compared to the costs of protecting unregistered work should a dispute arise.

the right to publish or exploit the work through business transactions, essentially the buying and selling of musical compositions.

An infringement of any of these rights entitles the copyright holder to take action for copyright infringement. Two factual elements are necessary to prevail in a copyright infringement action: a substantial similarity in the infringing work with the original work, and proof the infringing party had access to the original work.

SOURCES OF INCOME

From the exclusive rights granted by the copyright law arise the following four major sources of income for the copyright holder.

Mechanical income. A license issued for the use of the composition on a mechanical device, such as a CD, cassette, or DAT tape. The mechanical license fee is a statutory rate that also can be negotiated with the user. (The statutory rate is presently 6.95 cents/song per record sold for songs five minutes in length or less. 1.1 cents is added for each minute or fraction thereof that the song goes over five minutes.) This is the most identifiable and substantial source of income for copyright holders. A platinum album (1 million units sold) containing ten songs (five minutes or less in length) licensed at the full statutory rate generates $695,000 in mechanical royalties.

Performance income. These royalties are derived from the performance of compositions, including radio, television, restaurants,

and telephone "on-hold" music. Most musicians and publishing companies join performance rights societies and have these organizations license the use of their songs and collect the associated performance royalties.

Print income. When sheet music and compilations of printed versions of compositions are manufactured and sold, a royalty is earned by the copyright holder.

Synchronization income. Utilization of a composition in movie, video, or television programming requires a "sync license." This is a negotiated license based on a number of variables, including how much of a hit the song is, the duration of use, how the work is used, and who is using the composition. It is not unusual for a hit song utilized on a multi-year ad campaign for a major product to garner a six-figure fee for the sync rights alone. Note that this income is separate from the performance income, which is earned on top of the sync fee.

SIGNING OFF

Until the copyrights are transferred to a third party, they remain the exclusive rights of the original composer/copyright holder. The transactions of all of these rights and the income derived from them translate into the multi-million dollar industry of music publishing. This is the real big game in the music industry.

CHAPTER 26

The Name Game

Throughout the history of the music business, issues of trademarks have been hotly contested and at times hotly litigated. And if you think trademarks are something that only big corporations or successful bands have to worry about, you're wrong. Your small-time club act could be held legally accountable if it happens to tread inadvertently on a trade-marked band name. It's not exactly a prime career move to get slapped with a court order demanding that you cease and desist using your band's name and destroy all items—including the boxes of CDs that you slaved over—bearing the name in question.

WHAT IS A TRADEMARK?

Trademarks are marks such as names, logos, slogans, or particular type styles that identify the source of goods in the marketplace. The counterpart to trademarks for identifying the source of services (providing live entertainment services, for example) are servicemarks. Trademarks offer protection from competitors only in similar fields, which is why naming your band "Taurus" will not draw fire from the Ford Motor Company, as your band is selling music not automobiles.

Trademark law falls under the general body of law dealing with intellectual property. Before we proceed too far into a discussion of trademarks, it is important to distinguish trademarks from copyright.

Copyrights deal with the protection of rights that arise from the expression of ideas in tangible forms of media, such as paintings, songs, or recordings. Copyright law is often confused with trademark law because some copyrightable works, such as the Rolling Stones artwork depicting a pair of lips with a tongue sticking out, also serve as trademarks.

Trademarks, then, are those tangible forms of expression that the public identifies with the source of a specific product. "Strong" trademarks (such as the Stones' mouth and tongue logo or the typeface used by the Beatles) are ones that, when observed by a consumer, elicit recognition of a particular company or, in the case of musicians, an act. With merchandising revenues generating millions of dollars for bands, it is crucial to establish and protect a name and/or logo that identifies your act with the source of the artistic services being marketed to the public.

PICKING AND CHOOSING

Certainly one of the first orders of business after putting together a band is determining the group name. In order to establish a trademark, the proposed name must be fanciful, rather than descriptive. "Guitar Trio with Lead Vocalist" merely describes the source of the service; "That Slimey Mess" is fanciful. Most musicians actually do an informal, local trademark search simply by going through names with each other and determining if they have heard of other bands with that name playing around town.

When signing a record deal,
pay close attention to issues regarding the
name of your act.

Because trademarks are a "use it or lose it" proposition, you need to strengthen the trademark by getting the public to identify the group with the name. Playing gigs, releasing a record, getting press, and otherwise promoting the name will hopefully make the public aware of the name, and make the name synonymous with the act. The creation of a logo can be an important step in making the trademark even stronger. Unlike copyrights, which get immediate protection under the law, trademarks take time to develop because the public-recognition determines how strong the trademark is.

LEGAL LEGWORK

As with patents and copyrights, following certain legal formalities will help protect against trademark infringement. The first of these formalities is to file a fictitious business-name statement in the county in which the act does business. This usually requires filing forms with the county and doing a search of existing names in use. This filing establishes a public record and puts third parties on notice of the use of the name.

If the services being rendered by the act are expected to go beyond the city or county limits, the act should consider obtaining a state or federal trademark or servicemark. The qualifications and procedures vary from state to state, so I recommend contacting your state's Secretary of State. At the federal level, you need to prove that you have crossed state lines with your service (i.e., a band with records in stores in different states, a band with advertisements for gigs they have performed in different states, a production company advertising in magazines that have circulation in more than one state).

In addition, at both the state and federal levels, the party seeking the trademark must conduct a search to ensure that they are not infringing upon another party's trademark. This search is extremely important, not to mention tedious and time consuming. If you don't want to do the legwork yourself, trademark-search services are available. (You can usually find listings for them in your local *Yellow Pages.*) Prices for such searches vary from a couple hundred dollars to several thousand dollars, depending on the extent of the search and the desired detail of the report. In the music field, searches are made in phone books, professional publications, and in the Federal Registry, the giant database covering all registered trademarks.

When a trademark or servicemark is determined to be valid, has met the standards of being in interstate commerce, and has not infringed upon another trademark, it is then eligible to be a registered trademark or servicemark recognized under Federal law, signified by the "circle R."

INFRINGEMENT

Infringement occurs when, by using a certain trademark, a party promotes confusion in the

*Following certain legal
formalities will help protect against
trademark infringement.*

marketplace as to the source of the goods or services. This happens many times when a band splits up and the various factions attempt to use the band name to keep the initial group's loyal audience. A famous case that provided a great deal of the body of law regarding band names concerned the 1950s group The Platters, who broke up and subsequently flooded the public with a number of different versions of "The Platters," all singing the same songs at their gigs!

A variation on this theme is when an act has established a strong local trademark that is infringed by a major act using a similar name at a later date. This was the case when 1970s funk band Bootsy's Rubber Band was pursued by a smaller act called The Rubber Band that had established a prior use of the name. And in the mid 1980s, the supergroup Asia was issued a cease-and-desist order by a bar band with the same name. In order to play in the club band's geographical area, the supergroup had to pay them a hefty fee.

IT'S ALWAYS SOMETHING

When drafting a band partnership agreement, take great care in determining how the important asset of the band's trademarks and servicemarks are going to be handled. Will it be extinguished if two or more people leave the band? Can leaving members perform under the band name? What about merchandise revenue generated from the use of the band name? When signing a record deal, pay

close attention to issues regarding the name of your act. I have seen record companies actually gain ownership of a group name through language found in the recording contracts. (This name-ownership issue is rumored to be the reason the artist formerly known as Prince changed his name to a symbol.) Additionally, when entering into a record deal, you are warranting to the label that they will not encounter any problems by releasing your records, including your potential infringement of another act's trademarks.

Very few of us like to deal with legal issues, but by taking some important legal steps early in your band's existence, you can establish a strong trademark and use it to it's fullest advantage.

Music Contracts

The deal, the holy grail of ambitious dreamers, is a music-industry term that defines the bond between an artist and a record company, in which the artist's work is exploited for mutual profit. For those struggling to make a living playing music, the "deal" represents a catapult to stardom.

But business deals have a dark side, and what you don't know can hurt you. A bad contract sidetracks a career faster than a record without hits. Even superstars such as Bruce Springsteen and Tom Petty have experienced contract renegotiations that delayed them from releasing albums. While the actual contracts themselves can be pretty complicated, the basic legal tenets underlying most deals are pretty straightforward.

LET'S MAKE A DEAL

Let's review some basic contract law. A deal is an agreement; an agreement is a contract. In order for a contract to exist, it must exhibit three main components: an *offer*, an *acceptance* of the offer, and what is known in the legal field as *consideration* (the thing or promise being exchanged). A contract need not be in writing to be binding, but written agreements are much easier to prove and enforce.

Another important thing to understand is the *type* of deal you're seeking. Here's a look at the three most common music industry agreements.

EXCLUSIVE ARTIST AGREEMENT

The terms *record deal, production deal, development deal, all-in deal,* and *sign-here-and-we'll-make-you-a-star deal* usually are associated with exclusive artist agreements. These deals have a number of variations, depending upon the party (major label, independent label, independent producer, etc.) with whom the artist signs the contract. What is being traded is the artist's exclusive recording services for the purpose of making records. One of the major deal points is the length of the agreement. This is specified in terms of time (one year, plus four one-year options) or delivery of minimum recording commitments (five albums, with option periods commencing six months after each album is delivered).

Another major point is artist compensation. This is where artist royalties (and advances against those royalties) enter the picture. In exchange for the exclusive services of an artist, record companies pay a royalty based on units sold. Usually, this is a percentage of the record's suggested retail price. These figures, which differ greatly from deal to deal, are based on a number of variables ranging from the commercial stature of the artist to the willingness of the record company to bet on an artist's future sales. Although these variables make it difficult to ballpark standard figures, a new artist may be offered a royalty of less than ten percent of retail, while a mega-superstar can command more than twenty percent.

The bottom line of any business relationship is the element of trust between the artist and those charged with courting success.

Artist advances are royalty payments made up front (before a record even exists) and are recoupable by the record company from accrued royalties. In effect, the advance is a loan secured by the artist's future royalties. The recoupment (by the record label) of other costs, such as recording and video budgets, tour support, and promotional budgets are subject to negotiation. Again, the outcome of these negotiations depends upon the relative bargaining positions of the parties. A deal offering a $50,000 artist advance, a $100,000 recording budget, a $75,000 video budget, and $25,000 in tour support, logs $250,000 in recoupable monies. Assuming a ten percent royalty on albums listing at $10, an artist selling 200,000 units remains in debt to the record company and therefore is not entitled to royalty payments.

PUBLISHING AGREEMENTS

Songwriter rights probably are the most valuable rights in the music industry. At the root of multi-million dollar publishing and record company acquisitions are the up-and-coming songwriters who trigger the entire process by writing good songs. However, until the songwriter grants rights to a third party, he or she is self-published. This means the writer is the sole person who can pitch the song or grant other parties the right to exploit it.

As soon as rights are granted to a third party, various songwriter/publisher deals arise. Publishers obtain songs from writers for a specific period of time, during which the publisher attempts to place them. For example, a publisher might try to get your song cut by a current hit artist, or included on a movie soundtrack. In exchange for these services, publishers are entitled to a portion of the royalties generated by the song.

There are variations on this theme. Single-song deals limit the ties between the writer and publisher to a specific song. Sometimes the writer is paid a minor advance to cover demo costs, and the publisher is given a deadline to place the song. (Some songwriters secure a reversion of all rights granted the publisher if the song is not covered within the specified time.) Long-term publishing deals are subject to many of the same negotiating points as an exclusive artist deal, except the artist is bargaining with songs, rather than with phonograph records.

In recent years, it hasn't been unusual to see seven-figure publishing deals signed by successful artist/writers. When evaluating a publishing deal, artists should research their current market value and set contract demands based on the enthusiasm of company representatives.

MANAGEMENT AGREEMENTS

Behind every successful artist is a strong team consisting of a personal manager, business manager, lawyer, and booking agent. Agreements for personal and business management services are critical to an artist's career, as they

Behind every successful artist is a strong team consisting of a personal manager, business manager, lawyer, and booking agent.

are the cornerstone of a successful business team. The personal manager's agreement usually is multi-year, with compensation based on a percentage of the artist's income. (For an overview of how the artist-manager relationship works, see chapter 4, "Personal Managers.")

In the early, no-income stages of an artist's career, the manager often assumes multiple roles in return for future compensation. During this embryonic period (based almost solely on trust), care must be taken to negotiate fair agreements between the parties that set forth realistic goals, expectations, and objective standards of performance. These can include dollar incentives ("artist will be making $10,000 a year in the music business within one year") or specific goals ("artist will be signed to a major record label within one year"). It is difficult to negotiate these agreements because they require protection of both sides. For instance, if an artist outgrows a manager's capabilities, a settlement must be based on an intangible estimate of how far the artist would have gotten without the manager's efforts.

A business manager is enlisted when the artist begins to make money and major accounting and tax advice is needed. Legal counsel can be of help from the very beginning, as issues ranging from the formation of a musical group, to reviewing all of the aforementioned agreements, require the guidance of a lawyer who (hopefully) knows the business and cares about your music. The final member of the management team is the booking agent, who negotiates the artist's personal appearance agreements.

SUMMATION

This only touches on the basic business deals. It takes extensive study to understand the legal elements of music contracts. Leaving these "non-creative" machinations to your business team can be more trouble than reading a few books and consulting with music professionals. The bottom line of any business relationship is the element of trust between the artist and those charged with courting success. Why live in the dark? Educating yourself about major deals puts you on even ground with the executive on the other side of the table.

CHAPTER 28

Dissecting a Deal

I t's surprising that so many musicians can write complex harmonies, hard-wire and configure an entire MIDI studio, and play four different instruments but have no concept of how a record deal works. When it comes to record contracts, ignorance is *not* bliss. Entrusting your business fate to a contract's incomprehensible fine print could put your career in jeopardy.

Granted, a musician isn't required to know every single detail of how a deal works—that's what lawyers are for—but it is important to have a basic grasp of the language and major points of a deal. With that in mind, here is a clause-by-clause analysis of contract points to help alleviate the shock when your first 45-page record deal arrives at the door.

AN OVERVIEW

Before we tackle the specific components of a record deal, it is important to understand the overall scope of a contract. In short, a record company desires to hire the exclusive services of a recording artist for a period of time. During this contract period, the company records the artist's performances, manufactures the record, and distributes, promotes and sells it throughout a specified territory. In exchange for these services, and certain other rights that the artist grants to the record company, the artist is paid royalties based on the sales of the record. Simple? Yes. And by looking at the various provisions that make up this arrange-

ment, we can simplify it even further. Let's take a look at the common headings found in record deals.

Contract term. Because the record label is investing a great deal of money in production and promotion, they want the total of the contract periods to be as long as possible. One method of determining this term is to define it by an initial period of time (e.g., one year), plus a series of option periods. Another method of calculating the term of a contract is to use a triggering event, such as when a record is turned in (e.g., "The initial period and the subsequent option periods shall end on the last day of the twelfth month following Artist's delivery of the respective period's LP."). Using this method of calculation with a hypothetical initial year plus six options, if the artist takes nine months to write and record each album, the eventual total term could be in excess of ten years! Some states, such as California, actually put a limit on how long an artist may be kept under contract and have drafted legislation to protect artists in this regard.

Recording obligations. Record contracts call for a minimum number of singles and/or albums, as well as the timing of the delivery, depending on the marketing plan of the label and how they wish to introduce the artist to the marketplace.

Most artists entering into their first record deal are surprised by language stating that they are obligated to rerecord and redeliver material to make it "technically and commercially

*Publishing rights and merchandising rights
are still subject to separate negotiation, either with
the record company or third parties.*

satisfactory" to the record company. This is a major artistic leap of faith that artists must make prior to signing on the dotted line with a label. "Technically satisfactory" is an objective term; a series of engineers can always help the parties determine if a master is satisfactory for manufacturing records. On the other hand, an artist and record executive may be on completely different sides when it comes to determining what is "commercially satisfactory." For example, what if the artist is a folk guitar-picking singer/songwriter and the record exec feels this image is no longer "commercially satisfactory," thus requiring a "new disco-country-grunge record" to be delivered?

Recording budget. Artists need to be given a competitive budget to make a competitive record. Based on the production experience and how much equipment is necessary and/or owned by the artist, recording budgets can vary dramatically. For example, a solo singer/songwriter accompanying herself on acoustic guitar will not cost nearly as much as a 7-piece band with background vocalists, accompanied on some tracks by a full-sized symphony orchestra.

It is not unusual for recording budgets for first-time artists to exceed several hundred thousand dollars. Bear in mind that labels will try to include as much as possible in the recording costs, such as producer fees, transportation costs related to recording, all studio rental, etc. There is a down-side to the artist learning how to record and experimenting "on the label's tab," as all recording costs are recoupable by the label prior to royalties being paid to the artist.

Artist advances. By far the most publicized figures in the entertainment industry are the astronomical dollar amounts advanced to artists. While mega-stars are subject to multi-million-dollar advances when they move from label to label, first-time artists are rewarded with more modest and reasonable dollars up front.

Artist advances are simply royalties paid in advance to the artist against the label's "hunch" that the artist will not only recoup the advances but far exceed them. The amount of the advance is determined by a number of factors including (1) how developed and unique the act is, (2) how popular the act may be when coming into the deal, (3) who the group's management team is, and (4) whether or not other record labels are competing for the services of the act.

Advances for option periods are negotiated at the inception of a deal, when no one really knows how successful the act will be. Who could have predicted how big Madonna's third option period would have been worth before she began recording her first record? One solution is to base future advances on the success of prior records. For example, a contract could include language that says, "The artist advance for the first option period shall be the higher of $50,000 or 50 percent of the royalties earned by artist within the first nine months of the release of artists initial LP." In this scenario, if the artist

Artist advances are simply royalties paid in advance to the artist against the label's "hunch" that the artist will not only recoup the advances but far exceed them.

has an incredible hit record and earns $500,000 in royalties within the first nine months of sales, the option period advance will be $250,000 instead of $50,000. Note that an advance floor of $50,000 is built in to ensure that the artist will still receive an advance should the initial LP do only moderately well on the retail level.

Royalties. A major point of any deal is how much the artist will eventually be paid. Artists are paid a royalty based on the retail price of the record. The amount of this royalty varies dramatically from artist to artist, the range being from as low as 5 percent for an unknown artist to more than 20 percent for superstars.

The computation of the artist royalty is a major part of any negotiation. Often, several pages of a recording contract are devoted to setting forth the various reductions, deductions, and adjustments made to the basic royalty before money is paid to the artist. These can include packaging deductions (to pay for artwork and jewel boxes), sales outside of the country, sales on military bases, and sales of discount records.

While on the subject of royalties, the auditing provisions of an artist contract are important to mention here. Most agreements place specific restrictions on the artist as to when and how they can object to an accounting statement from the label or conduct an audit of the label. These must be closely monitored in order to preserve the rights to look for, find, and eventually recover "lost" royal-

ties later.

Recoupable costs. The record label is not simply giving money away to artists; the label wants to recoup all monies spent launching an artist prior to paying out any royalties. Although these costs are negotiable, they typically include all artist and producer advances, the entire recording budget, the video budget, tour support, third-party promotion fees, and related expenses. Adding all of these costs together, it is not unusual for artists to be in the red even after they have a gold record on the wall!

Grants of rights. Various rights are granted to a record company by an artist as part of an exclusive artist agreement. First and foremost is the right to own the master recordings made during the term of the agreement. Note that the right to own the master recordings (thus the copyright in the masters) is separate and distinct from the copyright in the songs on those masters. Without this ownership right, the record label is unable to freely reproduce and sell different configurations of records manufactured from the masters. Constitutionally, all persons have a right to privacy, so record contracts have specific grants from the artist to the label of the right to use photos, likenesses, biographical material, and the like in connection with the reproduction of the records.

Because the record company endeavors to freely market and exploit the records featuring the artist, contracts customarily require a grant of a power of attorney for the

The label wants to recoup all
monies spent launching an artist prior to
paying out any royalties.

label to stand in the artist's stead and execute documents (i.e., copyright forms, assignments, and license agreements connected with the label's ownership of the masters). Caution must be taken on the part of the artist to understand and limit the scope of this power of attorney. Although they are an exception, some unscrupulous executives have abused the right to sign various documents on an artist's behalf, leaving an artist penniless after generating a great deal of money for a label.

Videos. Issues surrounding the commitment to producing videos, video budgets and recoupments, artistic control of image by the artist, and the possible sale of videos or audio/video products are hot topics of negotiations. Because technology is evolving at such a great pace today, it is wise to be as specific as possible when negotiating the video aspects of a recording deal, holding back the rights for technology and products not yet in existence.

Promotion/tour support. A great record without promotional support serves only one purpose: taking up space in a warehouse or in record store. A clear promotional plan including a budget, give-away items, release strategy, independent radio and retail promotion, and tour support will go a long way in bolstering sales. One of the most important commitments a label can make to an act is underwriting a promotional tour. Note, however, that this is a recoupable expense and should be carefully planned to result in sales of records in order to justify the expense.

What the artist keeps. Given all of the above, it might seem that an artist retains very little when making a record deal. The reality is quite the contrary. Publishing rights and merchandising rights are still subject to separate negotiation, either with the record company or third parties. Although record companies may insist that inclusion of publishing and merchandising is a deal-breaker, it is increasingly common for the artist to retain these rights. Additionally, entering into a record deal is not a sell-off of any money an artist may make from live gigs, television appearances, endorsements, or other aspects of their careers.

If you're fortunate enough to get offered a recording contract, be sure to have your deal reviewed by a competent music attorney. But working with a lawyer doesn't excuse you from possessing a basic understanding of the terms of a standard record deal. That knowledge could prevent you from becoming an indentured servant to a label. The important factors in any contract negotiation are removing the fear factor, considering your legal options, and taking control of your professional destiny.

CHAPTER 29

The Rights Stuff

I f there's anything you've learned so far in reading this book, it's that the music business is downright complicated. There are deals to negotiate with record companies, publishers, and collaborators; copyrights to file and protect; and distributors to fight with. Even if you have no interest in getting involved in the corporate end of the business, you still have a lot of hurdles to clear if you want to release your music yourself.

But not everything related to the music industry is designed to make your life more difficult. Take performing rights societies, for example. These organizations exist to save you the hassle of monitoring how and where your songs are used. Most musicians have heard of these groups and are familiar with the acronyms ASCAP, BMI, and SESAC (respectively, American Society of Composers, Authors, and Publishers; Broadcast Music Inc.; and Society of European Stage Authors and Composers). These acronyms follow the songwriting credits on just about every CD or album in your collection. However, many musicians aren't familiar with what exactly these organizations do or how they do it.

THE BASICS

Holders of a particular copyright (e.g., a song) have five basic sets of rights: the mechanical rights, the right to make derivative works, the right to display the work, the publishing rights, and the right to perform the work. These rights roughly correlate to the breakdown of income generated by a copyrighted work. For example, a copyrighted song can generate the following types of income: *mechanical income,* which is the money made from the manufacture and sale of recordings of the song itself; *synchronization income* from songs used in sync with film, video, or other audio-visual presentations; *print income* for printed or sheet music; and *performance income,* a major source of income for songwriters and publishers, generated when anyone plays a copyrighted song, be it on radio or television or in a restaurant or nightclub.

By joining a performing rights society, a songwriter or publisher grants the organization permission to monitor airplay or other usages that his or her song receives and collect the appropriate license fee. (Members of performing rights societies are often referred to as *affiliates.*) The organization keeps a portion of the license fee for administrative costs and then divides the remainder between the songwriter and publisher. (If you act as your own publisher, then you get all the money.) ASCAP, BMI, and SESAC all have relationships with similar organizations in other countries; they collect and distribute income generated in the U.S. by foreign groups. These foreign organizations do the same for U.S. songs that get airplay abroad.

Each performing rights society has a membership department; don't be shy about contacting them to get the information you need to make your decision.

SIZING UP THE PLAYERS

Even though these organizations offer essentially the same services, they are not exactly alike. ASCAP and BMI are the largest performing rights societies, but in the past few years, SESAC has focused its efforts on becoming a more market-driven and service-oriented organization.

ASCAP, the oldest performing rights organization, was started in 1914 by songwriters and publishers who wanted to forge a coalition to enforce payment of performance royalties. The group now has more than 75,000 U.S. members and represents more than 200,000 foreign-society affiliates. To be a member, you must have a commercially recorded musical composition or one for which sheet music is commercially available. Publishers need to be regularly engaged in the music publishing business or have works that are performed by the society's licensees. ASCAP currently charges annual dues of $10 for writers and $50 for publishers.

BMI was founded in 1940, in response to ASCAP's resistance to licensing popular music (all three performing rights societies now license every genre). The organization represents the works of more than 160,000 songwriters, composers, and publishers. To be eligible for BMI membership, you must have written (or be the music publisher of) a musical composition that is either commercially published or recorded or otherwise likely to be performed. BMI charges no dues or initiation fees.

Contacting the Performing Rights Societies

ASCAP

New York office: tel. (212) 621-6000, fax (212) 724-9064

Los Angeles office: tel. (213) 883-1000, fax (213) 883-1049

Nashville office: tel. (615) 742-5000, fax (615) 742-5020

Chicago office: tel. (312) 472-1157, fax (312) 472-1158

e-mail info@ascap.com

Web www.ascap.com

BMI

New York office: tel. (212) 586-2000, fax (212) 245-8986

Los Angeles office: tel. (310) 659-9109, fax (310) 657-6947

Nashville office: (615) 401-2000, fax (615) 401-2707

Web www.bmi.com

SESAC

New York office: tel. (212) 586-3450, fax (212) 489-5699

Nashville office: tel. (800) 826-9996, fax (615) 329-9627

e-mail affil@sesac.com

Web www.sesac.com

Performing rights organizations also sponsor showcases, seminars, and workshops across the country.

When it was established in 1930, SESAC forged its niche by licensing only European and gospel performers. The society has expanded its coverage to all styles but maintains a division called SESAC Latina, which deals solely in performance rights for Spanish-language music. With 3,000 members, SESAC is the smallest of the three performing rights societies, and it is also the most selective about admitting new writers and publishers. Songwriters interested in joining SESAC must submit a recording of three original compositions (one of which must be written entirely by the applicant) with lyric sheets, and a listing of all current musical activity, such as performances, television appearances, and so on. The writer/publisher relations department decides whether to admit the applicant after reviewing the application and the submitted materials. This selection process stems from SESAC's desire to focus on what they call "a repertory based on quality rather than quantity." Even though the membership is small, SESAC has some pretty big-selling and well-known members: Cassandra Wilson, U2, Bob Dylan, and Bob Carlisle are all SESAC affiliates. The idea is that, with a smaller membership, the organization can give more individual attention to each affiliate. SESAC members pay no dues or initiation fees.

THE LAND OF THE FEE

Each performing rights society issues a blanket license to organizations such as television and radio stations, granting the licensees access to all songs in the society's repertoire. The license fee varies depending on the size of the listening audience. For example, a nightclub that holds 1,000 people will pay a lower fee than will a major metropolitan radio station that has hundreds of thousands of listeners.

The major licensees, again such as a metropolitan radio station, submit their play lists to the performing rights societies so the societies can then calculate the performance royalties. Furthermore, each society surveys radio stations, cable and network television, nightclubs, malls, amusement parks, and so on for song usage and then collects the corresponding fees. Each organization has its own surveying method and formula for determining how much play a song probably gets based on survey results. ASCAP, BMI, and SESAC each pay their members four times a year.

OTHER BENEFITS

In addition to tracking and collecting money for use of your songs, performing rights societies provide many other benefits to members. Most hold local talent showcases that are frequented by A&R reps looking for new talent. They also sponsor music-related seminars and workshops across the country, which is a great way to pick up new skills and connect with other musicians in your area.

ASCAP and BMI members have access to medical, dental, and life insurance as well as

The license fee varies depending on the size of the listening audience.

insurance for musical instruments and equipment. ASCAP, BMI, and SESAC all have comprehensive Web sites that offer information on the organizations, access to all the titles in their catalogs, and many other resources. For example, the ASCAP site has an annotated membership agreement (click on a highlighted term in the agreement and you get a full definition of that term), and the BMI site has extensive sections that deal with many of the common performing rights concerns of writers and publishers, including how collaborations between BMI and non-BMI writers work.

Clearly, there are many good reasons to join a performing rights society, especially if you plan to pursue a career in music. Choosing which organization to join is probably a little more difficult. Talk to other musicians and find out which organizations they've chosen and why. Also, each performing rights society has a membership department; don't be shy about contacting them to get the information you need to make your decision. The important thing is to start collecting the money that's due to you.

CHAPTER 30

A Brief Music-Business Glossary

I t's a horrible feeling when, part way through a negotiation, you begin to realize that you are speaking a different language from the executives on the other side of the table. Here are a number of key—and often misunderstood—music-business terms. Throughout these definitions, the term "artist" describes writers, recording artists, or producers (any person who creates the work that is being traded), and "company" refers to record, management, production, or publishing companies. (For a complete reference on this subject, check out *The Dictionary of Music Business Terms,* by Tim Whitsett, published by Mix-Books.)

Advance Moneys paid to an artist in anticipation of future earnings, such as recording or publishing royalties. Advances come in the form of *general artist advances,* which are cash payments to artists; *all-in advances,* which include recording budgets; and *third-party advances,* which are payments made to third parties on the artist's behalf, such as payments to record promoters. Although sometimes viewed as loans, advances are not repaid in the same manner as conventional loans because the company making the advance is taking a calculated risk that the advance will be repaid from royalties. For example, if a record does not sell well, the company must absorb the loss.

Budget The amount of money allocated by a company to complete a specific project. This is usually a major part of any contract negotiation because it sets the tone for the dollar commitment that a record label, independent production company, or artist is willing to risk in order to make a project happen. Because it affects the choice of recording studio and personnel, the size and allocation of a budget can have an impact on many of the creative decisions that will be made during a recording project.

Copublishing The sharing of publishing revenue with a writer. In a typical writer-publisher arrangement, the publisher pays the writer a royalty in exchange for ownership of a writer's songs. The publisher keeps the rest of the income. When a writer establishes his or her own publishing company and is able to negotiate a copublishing deal, the writer receives not only the writer's royalty but also a percentage of the publisher's royalty.

Cross-collateralization Using multiple royalties as collateral for advances. Many times, an artist brings multiple talents or rights to a record company (e.g., exclusive artist rights, musical compositions, exclusive merchandising rights), and the company will want to secure its entire investment in the artist with all of those rights.

For example, if the record company makes multiple deals with the artist for the various rights given above, the record company will try to use the publishing royalties to repay advances made against the artist deal—the future earnings serving as collateral for one deal are now crossing over into another deal. You should be careful to avoid cross-collateralization when drafting any agreements.

Some acts make more of their income from the sale of merchandise than they do from record sales or writing music.

Deductions Various items taken "off the top" from gross receipts prior to the payment of royalties to an artist. A great deal of time is devoted to the negotiation of deductions because they can severely reduce the "bottom line" if not kept in check. Examples of deductions include administrative fees; packaging deductions to pay for artwork, printing, and CD jewel boxes; collection fees paid to third parties; and legal fees incurred to secure third-party use of a song or master.

Escalations Additional royalties added to the base royalty, usually in exchange for future option periods or as a bonus based on sales. (A base royalty is a set rate on which earnings are determined.) As an example, an artist may negotiate a base rate of 10 percent of a recording's retail price with 0.5 percent escalations at the 500,000 and 1,000,000 sales levels. For records 1–500,000, the royalty rate is $1.50 per record (10 percent of a $15 record); for records 500,001–1,000,000 the rate is $1.575 per record; for records 1,000,001 and beyond, the rate is $1.65 per record.

Gross Usually assumed to mean all income from all sources, the term "gross" sometimes requires further definition in entertainment contracts. "Gross" often refers only to money actually received by a party, instead of money that is simply credited to a party. This would make a major difference, for example, in a management agreement wherein the manager is being paid 20 percent of the gross, and though $100,000 is being credited to the artist by a record company, they have only received $30,000 in cash. Based on their understanding of gross, the manager may argue that they be paid their $20,000 commission on the amount *credited* to the artist, leaving only $10,000 for the band to split up while they await further payment from their record company. (If there are four band members, that only amounts to $2,500 per person.)

Masters The recordings that are reproduced to manufacture phonograph records, CDs, cassettes, or other forms of recorded music. Although masters are distinguished from demo recordings, the line of demarcation between the two blurs as artists and producers gain the ability to deliver finished works to labels.

Merchandising The selling of merchandise displaying the names, logos, and likenesses of artists. We've all seen the plethora of T-shirts, caps, lunch boxes, and other items of various levels of taste at concerts, record stores, and department stores. Some acts—especially those that appeal to pubescents and prepubescents such as the Backstreet Boys or the Spice Girls—make more of their income from the sale of merchandise than they do from record sales or writing music.

Net Profits Money left over after the deduction of all agreed-upon costs. One of the most hotly negotiated and litigated points in entertainment agreements is the calculation of what constitutes "the net," and it should be scrutinized in all contracts. When negotiating any sort of deal, be forewarned to list exactly what costs are to be deducted

When a copyrighted work is purchased by a commissioning party, he or she is no longer considered the author or copyright holder of the work.

when determining what the net profits will be. Many artists have been disappointed to find, after selling hundreds of thousands of records, that managers, producers, lawyers, and the record label are all paid from the gross, leaving little or no royalties when the net profits are doled out.

Options The contract periods beyond the initial period of an agreement. A typical recording contract may offer a one-album deal with an option for three more albums if the first album is successful. In these instances, the exercising of such an option is usually solely at the discretion of the record label. Record contracts often specify the number of options, who has the right to exercise the options, and what obligations the options are based on (e.g., a certain sales plateau or payment of an option advance).

Per Diems Daily payments, intended to cover living expenses while an artist travels to work on a project. Per diems usually are discussed, for example, when a musician is going on a tour or a producer is traveling to work on a project.

Performing Rights Society Better known by their acronyms (e.g., ASCAP, BMI, and SESAC), these organizations license, collect, and distribute performance royalties generated from various sources, including radio and television airplay on behalf of songwriters and music publishers.

Points This is short for *percentage points,* usually discussed when a party participates in the royalties of a deal. A great deal of confu-

sion arises when the basis of the points is not clearly defined or understood by the parties involved. For example, if an agent shopping a record deal asks for "two points," does that mean he is is entitled to 2 percent of the retail price of the record, or 2 percent of what the artist is making from the deal? Given a $15 record and a 10 percent artist royalty, this is the difference between the agent receiving 30 cents per record and three cents per record—a major swing when it comes to receiving royalties.

Recoupable Expenses All expenses an artist has to "pay back" before royalties begin to accrue. Once again, if these expenses are not clearly defined, creative accounting could keep an artist from receiving money for a substantial period of time, even if his or her album has healthy sales. Some typical recoupable expenses include artist advances, recording budgets, third-party advances, promotional expenses, and other reasonable costs associated with the project. Clearly, one of the drawbacks would be having differing views of what "reasonable costs" are.

Reversion of Rights The return of certain rights to an artist that have been granted to a third party. The reversion of rights usually happens with either the termination of a relationship or the occurrence or nonoccurrence of a certain event. For example, in publishing agreements, some writers negotiate the reversion of their copyrights in musical works if the publishing company is unable to secure uses for the songs within a specified time.

A great deal of confusion arises when the basis of the points is not clearly defined or understood by the parties involved.

Work for Hire When a copyrighted work is purchased by a commissioning party, the artist providing the work does so as a work for hire, thus he or she is no longer considered the author or copyright holder of the work. All rights to the copyright of the work are owned by the commissioning party as if they had created the work themselves. Many writers and producers inadvertently provide their services as a work for hire and find out too late that they have given up all of their right to ownership and, consequently, the royalties to a third party.

Index